THE UNIVERSITY OF MICHIGAN
CENTER FOR JAPANESE STUDIES

MICHIGAN PAPERS IN JAPANESE STUDIES
NO. 6

SUKEROKU'S DOUBLE IDENTITY:
THE DRAMATIC STRUCTURE OF EDO KABUKI

Barbara E. Thornbury

Ann Arbor

Center for Japanese Studies
The University of Michigan

1982

Open access edition funded by the National Endowment for the Humanities/ Andrew W. Mellon Foundation Humanities Open Book Program.

Printed and bound by CPI Group (UK) Ltd, Croydon, CR0 4YY

ISBN 978-0-939512-11-9 (paper)
ISBN 978-0-472-12794-8 (ebook)
ISBN 978-0-472-90190-6 (open access)

TABLE OF CONTENTS

Acknowledgements

I would like to thank the Japan Foundation, Canada Council, and Killam Fund for Advanced Studies for supporting me in the research and writing of this work.

My thanks go especially to Professors Leon Zolbrod, Matsuo Soga, and Andrew Parkin of the University of British Columbia.

I am also very grateful to Professor Gunji Masakatsu of Waseda University, Hattori Yukio of the National Theater of Japan, Karen Brock of Princeton University, and Mayumi Sakuma of Ochanomizu University.

My deepest gratitude is to my husband, Don.

Introduction

This book is a study of traditional, Edo kabuki. Its aim is to show that the seemingly illogical double identity of the townsman, Sukeroku, and the samurai, Soga Gorō, in the play Sukeroku is a surviving element of what was once a complex and coherent structure based on a traditional performance calendar.

Kabuki was the principal dramatic form and a mainstay of urban popular culture during the Tokugawa period. A large number of the practices which characterized kabuki during that time are still carried on today. Many, however, were abandoned in the last half of the nineteenth century, when Japan embarked on her course of modernization.

Perhaps the most important practice to be left behind was strict adherence to a traditional theater calendar, or shibai nenjū-gyōji. The calendar consisted of four "seasons," corresponding to four major production periods. These were the kao-mise, or "face-showing," production beginning in the eleventh month of the lunar year; the spring or New Year production which followed in the first month; the bon festival in the seventh month; and the farewell production, which brought the theater year to a close in the ninth and tenth months. The calendar was generally the same in Edo and Kamigata (Kyoto-Osaka) kabuki, but there were differences in the dramatic conventions of the two regions. The focus of this work will be on Edo, which came to be the center of culture in the Tokugawa period. It is also the place that is associated with Sukeroku.

The calendar provided the framework of kabuki. Kabuki was composed of a series of relatively short plays which were arranged and even rearranged during each production period according to the dictates of dramatic convention (especially those connected with seasonal change) and audience response. Kabuki was not regarded as a random collection of single plays, but rather, plays were seen as standing within the framework of the traditional calendar as a whole. The calendar was so crucial that unless its role is understood aspects of certain plays that survive in the present-day repertory, such as the double identity in Sukeroku, do not make sense.

Sukeroku is a major work of kabuki. Performed for the first time in 1713 by Ichikawa Danjūrō II, it flourishes today as one of the jūhachi-ban, or "eighteen favorites." Thus, the history of Sukeroku spans more than two hundred and fifty years, beginning when kabuki was just emerging as a major dramatic art form and continuing until the present when it is being kept alive by Japanese awareness of and reverence for great art forms of the past.

To show how the calendar functioned and what Sukeroku's double identity signifies, the book is divided into two parts. Part One studies the structure of Edo kabuki. The first chapter, which outlines that structure, is based for the most part on writings of the Tokugawa period. The second chapter then looks at the concepts of sekai, "tradition," and shukō, "innovation." Kabuki was the product of material that had become a familiar part of Japanese culture by repeated use and dramatization over long periods of time, starting before kabuki began, and material that was relatively new and was used to transform the older, set material. The double identity in Sukeroku came about as a result of this interplay between what was received by way of tradition and what was added by way of innovation.

Part Two considers the significance of the double identity. I conclude that Sukeroku's double identity gave Edo audiences a hero who was an idealization of the contemporary Tokugawa townsman and at the same time a transformation of a samurai god-hero of the past. The first chapter of Part Two traces the development of Sukeroku's Soga Gorō/samurai identity, from its origins in the early dramatic forms of nō, kōwaka, and ko-jōruri, to the representation of Soga Gorō in kabuki by Ichikawa Danjūrō I. The second then looks at the transformation of Soga Gorō into Sukeroku by discussing the origins of Sukeroku and its introduction to Edo kabuki by Ichikawa Danjūrō II. In Part Two, the discussions of kabuki are limited to Ichikawa Danjūrō I and his son, Danjūrō II, since their work was the basis of all later developments.

PART ONE: EDO KABUKI

Chapter 1

THE CALENDAR OF KABUKI

During the Tokugawa period kabuki was annually divided into four major production periods, comprising altogether about two hundred days of performance time.[1]

PRODUCTION	STARTING DATE
kao-mise ("face-showing")	11th month, 1st day
spring	1st month, 15th day
bon (refers to bon festival)	7th month, 15th day
farewell	9th month, 9th day

Strictly speaking, two more periods can be added: the third-month and fifth-month productions, beginning, respectively, on the third day of the third month and the fifth day of the fifth month. These, however, were usually part of the long-run spring production and will be treated as such here.

Opening the Theater Year: The Kao-mise Production

The theater year opened on the first day of the eleventh month, two months before the civil new year. No one knows for certain why this schedule was adopted, but it may go back to an historical relationship between drama and the agricultural cycle. Customarily, the eleventh month is the time to offer newly-harvested rice to the heavenly deities.[2] In Japan, as elsewhere, the mythological beginnings of drama are in offerings to the gods. Thus, kao-mise, which began with three days of ceremonial dance-dramas, may be regarded as a successor of these ancient offerings to the gods.

1. Hattori Yukio, Kabuki no genzō (Tokyo: Asuka Shobō, 1974), p. 153.
2. See Engi-Shiki: Procedures of the Engi Era, translated by Felicia Gressitt Bock (Tokyo: Sophia University, 1970), I, p. 97.

Actors of the Tokugawa period held one-year contracts with licensed theaters, and kao-mise was the first production after the settling of new contracts. This was the time for members of a newly-organized company to "show their faces" so that audiences could assess their potential for the coming year. Accordingly, the production was designed to display the company to its best advantage. To ensure that this was done the fullest possible dramatic program was planned, making kao-mise "the soul of kabuki."[3]

As the theater new year, kao-mise was a festive occasion. For the three days of opening ceremonies audiences gathered early in the morning to watch the manager of the theater perform the principal role of the venerable old man Okina in Shiki Sambasō.[4] His heir and another relative or an apprentice played the supporting roles of Senzai and Sambasō. This auspicious drama was the theater management's way of demonstrating support for the company.

Shiki Sambasō is a variation of Okina, an ancient drama that is also found in but predates nō. Okina represents a god in human form.[5] He is a symbol of longevity and was invoked at the accession of a new emperor to ensure successful rice-growing cycles during the reign.[6] In the Tokugawa period, when nō was the official ceremonial entertainment of the samurai class, a day's performance of nō was arranged according to a pattern of "five

3. kabuki no seimei. Hattori, Kabuki no kōzō (Tokyo: Chūō Kōron Sha, 1970), p. 161. The importance of this production is indicated by the fact that it was on a kao-mise playbill in 1680 that Tominaga Heibei had his name inscribed as "playwright" (kyōgen-tsukuri), thus becoming the first person to be so recognized. Prior to that there had been no special recognition of those who had contributed to the composition of kabuki plays. In Tominaga Heibei's time it was usual for kabuki actors (such as Heibei himself) to compose their own plays. As time went on, playwrighting became a full-time occupation for professionals. See Ted Takaya, "An Inquiry into the Role of the Traditional Kabuki Playwright," unpublished dissertation, Columbia University, 1969.
4. Shōkadō Hajo, Shibai nenjū-gyōji (1777; reprinted in Kyōgen sakusha shiryō-shū (1): Sekai kōmoku, shibai nenjū-gyoji, Tokyo: Kokuritsu Gekijo, 1974), p. 94. In Edo, the head of a theater was also the hereditary holder of the theater license. Their names were Nakamura Kanzaburō (Nakamura-za), Ichimura Uzaemon (Ichimura-za) and Morita Kan'ya (Morita-za).
At times other than kao-mise and New Year's Shiki Sambasō was performed by low-ranking actors (bandachi). See Gunji Masakatsu, Kabuki, translated by John Bester (Palo Alto: Kodansha, 1969), p. 52.
5. Inoura Yoshinobu, A History of Japanese Theater I: Up to Noh and Kyogen (Tokyo: Kokusai Bunka Shinkokai, 1971), p. 17.
6. See Ibid., p. 50.

steps plus Okina" (Okina-tsuki go-ban-date), meaning that one play from each of the five dramatic categories of nō was given, preceded by Okina.[7] In principle, this arrangement was not unlike that of kabuki.

During kao-mise Shiki Sambasō was followed by a waki-kyōgen, or auspicious "god play," the concept and terminology of which were probably borrowed from nō. Because each kabuki theater had its own waki-kyōgen, producing them was an expression of the pride of the theater. Examples include: Shuten Dōji at the Nakamura-za, Shichi-fukujin at the Ichimura-za, and Fukujin-asobi and the Morita-za.[8] Both Shiki Sambasō and waki-kyōgen were reserved for only the most special occasions, such as kao-mise, New Year's, and the opening or reopening of a theater building.

Because nō had a considerable influence on the early development of kabuki, it is natural to find features of resemblance in the two arts. Moreover, by preserving Okina (in the form of Shiki Sambasō), for example, kabuki, which was viewed by the samurai (especially those who considered themselves proper Confucianists) as a rather undesirable activity of the commoners, could create a symbolic association with recognized and accepted conventions.

Starting on the fourth day of the new theater year, the dramatic portion of kao-mise was presented. It had two major sections, which can be subdivided as follows:[9]

> I. First Section
>   a. Opening
>   b. Second step
>   c. Third step
>   d. Fourth step
>   e. Fifth step
>   f. Sixth step ──────► end[10]

---

7. Gondō Yoshikazu, Nō no mikata (Kyoto: Tōyō Bunka Sha, 1975), pp. 53-54. The five categories of nō plays are generally given as works concerning gods, warriors, women, made persons, and concluding works.
8. Shōkadō, Shibai nenjū-gyōji, p. 94.
9. Based on Hattori's analysis in Kabuki no kōzō, pp. 193-94, and Takamura Chikuri, E-hon shibai nenjū-kagami (1803; reprinted in Shibai nenjū-gyōji shū, Tokyo: Kokuritsu Gekijō, 1976), pp. 228-29.
10. Depending on the work, the end of the first section (the ō-zume) might come after the fourth step (and thus be equivalent to a fifth step) or after the fifth step (and thus be equivalent to a sixth step).

II. Second Section[11]
g. Sewa scene
h. Grand finale

In b. through f., the word "step" is the same as that used to describe the arrangement of nō. In fact, with the exception of g., the structure is described simply in terms of consecutive steps. In Japanese "to compose a play" (kyōgen o tateru) connotes building something step by step.

The opening and second step of the first section were staged early in the morning as warm-up exercises. They were composed by low-ranking playwrights and performed by low-ranking actors.[12] The opening was often comic, featuring unusual characters, such as animals and other-worldly beings. The second step would often be a dance piece and the plot might concern the unmasking of conspirators.[13]

Following the opening and the second step, the featured portion of the program began with the third step, which, during kao-mise, traditionally entailed a performance of the play Shibaraku. This play, like Sukeroku, is one of the "eighteen favorites" of kabuki. Its presentation during kao-mise was started by Ichikawa Danjūrō II in 1714.[14] What is now considered the established text of the play, however, dates only from 1895. Prior to that, Shibaraku was newly written every year, illustrating an important feature of kabuki dramatic practice: the exact same play was not performed twice. The basic situation remained fixed, but the identities of the characters and certain elements of plot were changed.

As the day progressed and the size of the audience increased, the work of higher-ranking playwrights and actors was performed. For both the leading playwright and actors, and the audience as well, the focus of kao-mise was its second section, usually a work with a strong seasonal association (the action

11. In the Kamigata area the first section was called the "beginning section" (mae-kyōgen) and the second section was called the "end section" (kiri-kyōgen). Unlike Edo kabuki structure, however, the Kamigata "beginning" and "end" sections were unrelated to each other. Gunji Masakatsu, Kabuki nyūmon, new ed. (Tokyo: Shakai Shisō Kenkyūkai Shuppan-bu, 1962), p. 139.
12. Takamura, E-hon shibai nenjū-kagami, p. 228.
13. Hattori, Kabuki no kōzō, p. 193, and Takamura, E-hon shibai nenjū-kagami, pp. 228-29.
14. Previously, Danjūrō I had performed Shibaraku sometimes in the first month and sometimes in the fifth month of the year. Kabuki jūhachi-ban shū, ed. Gunji Masakatsu, Nihon koten bungaku taikei, 98 (Tokyo: Iwanami Shoten, 1965), p. 30.

often took place in falling snow) and on a topical theme. This was in contrast to the first section, which was based on a long-established theme.

A requirement of Edo kabuki in general was that the first and second sections be linked together, even though they differed in style and substance. In order to achieve this link, in the course of the second section one or more characters revealed that they were really characters from the first section who had undergone a change of identity.[15] Moreover, the requirement of linking was also observed among the parts within the first and second sections.

The day ended with the grand finale, which brought the performance to a splendid conclusion. Elaborate dance-dramas were staged. The curtain was finally drawn at dusk (the performance having started at sunrise), with the announcement "That's all for today" (Mazu konnichi wa kore-giri).[16] This implies that if there was more time the performance would have gone on longer. A performance, in fact, did not end so much as it was cut off; the word for finale, ō-giri, literally means "great cutting-off." This is quite different from the tie-up-all-the-loose-ends conclusion we expect in Western drama.[17]

Kao-mise ran until the tenth day of the twelfth month, for about a month and a half altogether. Just as the play began in a ceremonial way, so too did it end that way with the "final dance" (mai-osame).[18] This entailed the presentation of Senshūraku, a dance with a chanted accompaniment, which was originally derived from the ancient art of gagaku. Most often used in the form it is given at the end of the nō play Takasago, Senshūraku is still used on various felicitous occasions, and in the case of kabuki was like a service of thanksgiving for a successful beginning to the theater year. The rest of the twelfth month was occupied with preparations for New Year's and the start of the spring production.

15. Kabuki kyakuhon shū, ed. Urayama Masao and Matsuzaki Hitoshi, Nihon koten bungaku taikei, 54 (Tokyo: Iwanami Shoten, 1961), p. 4.
16. Kore-giri (not kiri) is the proper reading. See Kabuki jūhachi-ban shū, ed. Gunji, p. 133.
17. Performances continued for about thirteen hours each day. For information on time restrictions, see Hattori, Kabuki no genzō, p. 6. It was not until the Meiji period that performances were permitted at night. See Gunji, Kabuki to Yoshiwara (Tokyo: Awaji Shobō, 1956), p. 49.
18. Takamura, E-hon shibai nenjū-kagami, p. 230.

The Long-Run Spring Production: The Soga Tradition

If kao-mise was the soul of kabuki, the spring production, which started in the first month, the beginning of spring on the lunar calendar, was its heart. It was a celebration not only of the cyclical renewal of life, but of the heroic Soga brothers whose tale of filial piety and revenge was the traditional basis of spring dramas. The relationship between the Soga brothers' tale and kabuki is a special one. The tale has provided much material for kabuki, and in many ways its themes and characters define kabuki.

In 1709 a Soga play was given as the spring production in three of the four theaters of Edo. The Yamamura-za, which had yet to be closed, did Aizen Soga, the Ichimura-za put on Meiseki Soga, and Fukubiki Soga was done at the Morita-za.[19] These productions, which came at a time when kabuki was still developing as a dramatic art form, were so successful that until the end of the Tokugawa period Soga plays were performed at all theaters in the spring.

New Year Observances

Like kao-mise, the spring production began in a ceremonial way, which of course included special New Year observances. Although the spring play did not open until the fifteenth day of the first month,[20] theaters were active from New Year's day. On the first day of the new year there was an opening ceremony consisting of Shiki-sambasō, the reading of a scroll by the head actor giving the titles of the upcoming work and a list of actors and their roles, and finally colorful New Year dances, such as Manzai and Harugoma, performed by young actors and accompanied by musicians in formal dress. Afterwards, actors made New Year calls at the teahouses which played an important supporting role in the kabuki world.[21] Theater economics required such calls, but there was also an element of family tradition involved as well. Even though actors were under contract to theaters, they behaved as if they were part of a family. As a family they made New Year visits, and when other families in society were sharing the mirror-shaped rice cakes that are a New Year tradition (on the eleventh day of the first month), within the theater they did the same. The confucian ideal of a society based on family relationships was a reality within the kabuki world, where every observance of the ceremonial year was performed as rigorously as in society at large.

19. Ihara Toshirō, Kabuki nempyō (Tokyo: Iwanami Shoten, 1956), I, p. 379.
20. "Little New Year" (ko-shōgatsu).
21. Takamura, E-hon shibai nenjū-kagami, pp. 189-90.

The Changing Spring Production

If conditions were favorable the spring production lasted upwards of six months, actually extending through the summer, which began in the fourth month of the lunar year. This is not to say, however, that the dramatic content remained the same throughout. Kabuki structure was such that as time passed parts of the production were modified or taken out completely and new parts added. The spring production was given a single overall title, which invariably included the word "Soga."[22] Titles were also given to designate changes made in the spring production. Sukeroku yukari no Edo-zakura, for example is the name of a part of Edo murasaki kongen Soga done in the third month of 1761 at the Ichimura-za. Many difficulties arise in identifying the works of kabuki because of the existence of overall titles as well as titles for separate parts of productions.

What determined the manner and extent to which changes were made in the long spring production? The answer involves seasonal and financial factors.

With the approach of the summer solstice, which could occur as early as the beginning of the fifth month of the lunar year, and the accompanying increase in daylight hours, more material could be presented and the production accordingly lengthened. Until the end of the Tokugawa period giving plays at night was prohibited. Curfew and social control aside, this had the practical effect of eliminating the use of torches to light the stage and thus reduced the terrible threat of fire that constantly plagued the city of Edo.

Besides more daylight hours for performances, plays were changed or added to by the tradition that dictated that plays reflect the changing seasons. As the New Year gave way to the mid-spring festivals and as these in turn gave way to the observances of summer, modifications were made in both dramatic content and theatrical presentation. The appearance of Sukeroku about the third month on a stage lavishly decorated with cherry blossoms was in harmony with the season. The chorus sings:

22. For example, Shikirei yawaragi Soga (Nakamura-za, 1716), Otoko-moji Soga monogatari (Nakamura-za, 1749), and Edo murasaki kongen Soga (Ichimura-za, 1761).

In springtime hazes,
    Blooms pink as Mount Yoshino fill Yoshiwara.
Tender shoots and gentle buds flourish in our view
    Of the Mountain Entrance House and the Three Harbors,
    Where the bursting cherries of Edo flower.[23]

Matters of money were naturally of great concern to theater owners. Financial backing had to be obtained, often through the agency of teahouses, in order to begin a production. The success of a production was then measured in box office receipts. No matter what the cost of opening a production, it could close any time if audience response was insufficient. If a kabuki production was not doing well and change was necessary, the actor was secure because he had a year-long contract. It was the play itself that somehow had to be changed.

In sum, a structure was required that could accommodate expansions in performance time, dramatic traditions associated with seasonal change, and the vagaries of box office success. Each of these requirements could be met because kabuki had a flexible, multi-part structure. When performance time became longer, more parts could be added. When a new season or lack of success required change, this could be done as well. Because many variables were involved, it is difficult to generalize about the structure. And it is this difficulty in generalization, arising from its characteristic flexibility, that has caused some to conclude that kabuki lacks a coherent structure.

The Spring Production in Outline

The following outline of the spring production will assume optimum audience response and financial conditions. Factors—such as the death of an actor, a fire, censorship—could prevent a production from continuing or even opening "on time," in the sense of beginning on the traditional starting date. In such cases, the order of the kabuki calendar was still adhered to as closely as possible, even if it meant some rearrangement of the schedule. In the year 1713 both the Yamamura-za and the Morita-za began kao-mise productions during the first month as well as during the eleventh month. In 1712 neither theater had a kao-mise production (the Nakamura-za's began on the fifteenth day of the twelfth month).[24] Although it appears that the Morita-za continued with its belated kao-mise production through the spring, the

23. "Sukeroku: Flower of Edo," in Kabuki: Five Classic Plays, translated by James R. Brandon (Cambridge: Harvard University Press, 1975), p. 56.
24. Ihara, Kabuki nempyō, I, pp. 408-10.

Yamamura-za went into a spring/third-month production in the third or fourth month (it is not certain which) with the play Hana-yakata Aigo-zakura, which contained the first Sukeroku.

The First and Second Months: New Year's

During the time allotted for the spring production in the first month of the year (a period of about two weeks, because the production began on the fifteenth day of the month, which corresponded to the "little New Year" of the civil calendar), only the first section was produced. After introductory presentations, the main portion of the first section began with the third step, as in the case of the kao-mise production, and continued through the fourth step, the fifth step, and an end step.[25]

The precise content of the third, fourth, and fifth steps differed depending on the play, but the story generally concerned the loyalty of Oniō Shinzaemon, his brother Dōzaburō, and Oniō's wife toward the Soga brothers, and their efforts to help the brothers carry out their revenge on their enemy Kudō Suketsune. This was followed by Taimen ("The Confrontation"), which brought the first month of the spring production to a climactic conclusion. Taimen is the dramatization of the Soga brothers' first meeting with Suketsune. In fact, a reason the spring production began on the fifteenth day of the first month is that it is the anniversary of the actual taimen.[26] Taimen was a dance piece, featuring fantastic aragoto poses, which wordlessly express the clash of the foes. An example of a surviving work which contains all these parts is Nenriki yatate no sugi, performed for the first time in the first month of 1806 at the Nakamura-za.[27]

At the end of Taimen in the text of Nenriki yatate no sugi, Sukenari (Soga Gorō) says: "Now the second section begins," indicating that it was time to proceed with the next part of the spring production. This line was inserted on the first day of the horse in the second month, which was also the day of the Inari shrine festival, which was celebrated in the theaters.

The Inari festival was celebrated with much gaiety both within and without the theaters. In the theaters the activities focused on the lower-

25. Atsumi Seitarō, Kabuki nyūmon (Tokyo: Tōkai Shobō, 1949), p. 123.
26. Gunji Masakatsu, Namari to suigin (Tokyo: Nishizawa Shoten, 1975), p. 15.
27. Text of play in Soga kyōgen gappei-shū, Vol. 14 of Nihon gikyoku zenshū (Tokyo: Shun'yōdō, 1929), pp. 1–140.

ranking actors who were collectively called "Inari town." The Inari shrine, guarded by a pair of foxes who are messengers of the Inari deity, was the tutelary shrine of these actors. On the festival day actors of Inari town set up an Inari shrine near the stage. The highest ranking actor took the role of the priest who carried out the celebration, which included a feast of fish and sake which all theater personnel would share.[28] It was appropriate that theaters specially marked this day, since the Inari shrine is where business people, among others, pray for prosperity. Large audiences were expected at the theater on the festival day. If the box office prospered the spring production could be extended considerably beyond the second month.

The Third and Fourth Months: The Flower Months

Starting on the third day of the third month (the peach festival), the spring production underwent further change. It was the season of blossoms, and the production had some connection with flowers in content and designation of subtitle. The stage, moreover, was decorated appropriately.

The third month was a busy one. A day was set aside when the theater management provided beautiful flower arrangements and a banquet to celebrate the success of the year thus far and to thank everyone for their cooperation and efforts. It was also a day for special song recitals and poetry composition. Also, on the fifteenth day representatives of the theaters visited shrines in and around Edo.[29] Moreover, the third month was also when servants in the residences of the daimyō in Edo had a holiday, and theaters could count on their attendance. To appeal to their interest, plays on the theme of feudal family rivalry, such as Kagami-yama and Sendai-hagi, were worked into the Soga play.[30]

Changes made in the spring production at this time varied year by year, but one or two parts were usually added or replaced.[31] From the fourth month on the structure of the spring production became less definite, because as the heat of summer increased audiences dwindled.[32] One expedient for

28. Shōkadō, Shibai nenjū-gyōji, p. 88.
29. Ibid., p. 89.
30. See Atsumi Seitarō, "Soga kyōgen no hensen to kanshō," Engeki-kai, 8, No. 2 (1950), 16–17.
31. See Mimasuya Nisōji, Sakusha nenjū-gyōji (1852; reprinted in Kabuki, Vol. 6 of Nihon shomin bunka shiryō shūsei, Tokyo: San'ichi Shobō, 1973), p. 678.
32. Ibid., p. 679.

drawing a crowd was to produce "one-night pickles" (ichiya-zuke), which were instant dramatizations of current events, particularly love-suicides. Hastily composed, most "one-night pickles" were not of high quality and their popularity was short lived.

The Fifth and Sixth Months: The Soga Festival

Final changes in the spring production were made on the fifth day of the fifth month, the day of the iris festival. As in homes throughout Japan, special baths with iris leaves floating on the water, thought to promote good health, were set up in the theaters on the festival day and enjoyed by theater personnel.

The most important day of the fifth month was the twenty-eighth, the anniversary of the Soga brothers' revenge. In each theater the long-run spring production culminated in a Soga festival which, by honoring the heroic brothers, at the same time gave thanks for the support that enabled the productions to come to a successful conclusion. The festival began in the middle of the fifth month and was marked by decorations in the theaters and by dances and comic performances which changed daily. The principal festival day was, of course, the twenty-eighth, when a more serious atmosphere prevailed.

The long-run spring production was formally brought to an end on the seventh day of the sixth month. Theaters then recessed for summer, until the start of the bon production. During this recess top-ranking actors went to summer resorts to escape the heat of the city. Second-rank actors toured the provinces as players in road shows, both in order to be out of the city and to supplement their incomes. During this period, too, necessary repairs were carried out on theater buildings. Theaters were also used by younger or lower-ranking actors who remained behind in Edo. They performed "summer plays," mainly practice performances. Audiences were sparse and ticket prices were cheaper than usual.

Winding Down the Theater Year: The Bon and Farewell Performances

The kao-mise and spring productions were the principal productions of the theater year. The bon production was important more because it coincided with a major celebration than because of the dramas presented. The season of bon is when spirits of the dead are said to visit the world of the living and when prayers and ceremonies are carried out in their honor. Unlike the spring production, which had a fixed starting point (the fifteenth day of the first month), the scheduling of the bon production was not so precise. Ideally, it began on the fifteenth day of the seventh month. Lingering heat, however, often discouraged top-ranking actors and audience members from returning to theaters at that time, making elaborate plans for the production unnecessary. Summer practice plays were frequently continued well into the eighth month. If new material was needed, plays adapted from the puppet theater could be used. After the end of the eighteenth century, newly written pieces were commonly used for the bon production.

In the eighth month decisions were made on changes in the company for the next season. This was done so that departing actors could plan for the farewell production, and also so that preparations for that dramas for the following theater year could begin. In order to compose plays, dramatists had to know which actors would be playing the parts.

Despite the rather informal nature of the dramatic program the highlight of the eighth month in the theaters was the moon-viewing celebration. On the evening of the fourteenth day stages were decorated with pampas grass and on the night of the fifteenth, the night of the full moon, there were banquets.

Farewell Production

The farewell production began on the ninth day of the ninth month, the day of the chrysanthemum festival. The production featured departing actors, especially those returning to troupes in Kyoto and Osaka. What was presented differed depending on the year and the theater.

As the old year came to an end, work on the new one began. On the evening of the twelfth day of the ninth month, the manager, head playwright, and leading actors of each of the kabuki theaters in Edo met to decide their program of plays for the upcoming year. Competition among the theaters was intense, and the meetings were held in utmost secrecy in selected tea houses. Lanterns decorated with the crests of popular actors were hung throughout the tea house district that evening, signifying the importance of the occasion.

The farewell production and the theater year concluded around the fifteenth day of the tenth month. The ceremony to welcome the new actors of a troupe took place two days later, on the seventeenth.

*   *   *

The traditional calendar gave kabuki the framework of its dramatic structure and the rhythm of its drama. The framework was the cycle of the ceremonial year and the rhythm was the regular passage of the seasons, months, and days within the year. Similarly, within the seasons the succession of months—especially during the long period of the spring production—provided natural points for adjusting the contents of plays.

Chapter 2

THE PRINCIPLES OF EDO KABUKI

Edo kabuki possessed an artistic structure that preserved long-standing cultural traditions, while at the same time renewing and updating them by means of innovation. In this chapter I will consider this characteristic interweaving of traditional and innovative material in Edo kabuki.

The Multi-part Structure of Kabuki

The multi-part structure, which gave kabuki its great flexibility, had its beginnings in the dances and comic sketches of early kabuki.[1] These are usually categorized as hanare-kyōgen, or "separate plays," as opposed to the later tsuzuki-kyōgen, or "continued plays." Tsuzuki-kyōgen appeared after authorities suppressed kabuki and closed all theaters in 1652 for violation of laws prohibiting homosexual prostitution. (Up to that time kabuki had been largely a prostitutes' art.) Theaters were allowed to reopen only on the condition that various changes in staging and in dramatic form and content be made.[2] One of the results of this ruling was that it stimulated the

1. Early kabuki includes the periods of women's (onna), young men's (wakashu), and the first decade of mature men's (yarō) kabuki.
  Women's kabuki flourished during the first quarter of the seventeenth century, until women were banned from the stage in 1629. Young men's kabuki started during the time of women's kabuki. It especially flourished during the administration of the third shōgun Tokugawa Iemitsu in the mid-seventeenth century. This period of kabuki ended when young men were banned from the stage. Mature men's kabuki followed and continues to the present day.
2. It was ruled that kabuki had to become monomane kyōgen zukushi, which means something like "a more fully developed representational dramatic art form." See Kawatake, Nihon engeki zenshi, p. 290. In his Kabuki-shi no kenkyū, Kawatake calls the development of kabuki rebyū-shiki no buyō kara sha-jitsu-teki na serifu-geki e ([a movement] from revue-type dance-drama to realistic drama), p. 383.

17

development of kabuki dramatic structure, leading eventually to the appearance of the sophisticated, multi-part tsuzuki-kyōgen form.[3]

The first plays with a multi-part structure of which we have any record were performed in 1664.[4] One is Hinin no kataki-uchi, attributed to the actor-playwright Fukui Yagozaemon (fl. 1660-1690), and performed in Osaka at the Araki Yojibei-za. The other is Imagawa shinobi-guruma, attributed to the actor-playwright Miyako Dennai (dates unknown), and performed in Edo at the Ichimura-za. It is noteworthy that the form appeared in the same year in both major centers of kabuki.

Without extant texts it is difficult to know what these plays were like.[5] What interest us here, though, is that they were both labeled as either two- or three-part plays (ni- or san-ban tsuzuki-kyōgen), depending on the source of information. It is tempting to use the terminology of Western drama and simply define a two-part play, for example, as a work in two "acts" or two "scenes," but this can be misleading. A part of a kabuki play was neither an act nor a scene in the sense that acts and scenes are divisions of a play that usually cannot stand independently. The parts of a kabuki play might in themselves be complete and potentially independent dramas.[6]

By the Genroku era the three-part play structure had become standard in the Kamigata area, and the four- or five-part structure standard in Edo.[7] There could, however, be more, or even fewer, than three, four, or five parts

After 1652 (when young men were banned from the stage), kabuki became known as kyōgen. Kyōgen, of course, originally referred to the contemporary-set, often comic plays that were part of the traditional nō program. Calling kabuki kyōgen was symbolic of the fact that kabuki was being forced to become more acceptable in the eyes of the authorities—and of society at large. Today the word kyōgen generally refers to any type of play.
3. Hattori argues that even without the stimulation of governmental edicts, kabuki would have developed a more sophisticated structure as a matter of course. Hattori, "Kabuki: kōzō no keisei," in Kabuki, Vol. 8 of Nihon no koten geinō, ed. Geinō-shi Kenkyūkai (Tokyo: Heibonsha, 1971), p. 45.
4. All evidence, unfortunately, dates from after the Genroku era. Ibid., p. 47.
5. Watsuji Tetsurō has tried to reconstruct these works by basing his efforts on later adaptations. Watsuji, Nihon geijutsu-shi kenkyū: kabuki to ayatsuri-jōruri (Tokyo: Iwanami Shoten, 1971), p. 469.
6. Hattori, "Kabuki: kōzō no keisei," p. 47.
7. Gunji, Kabuki, in Iwanami kōza: Nihon bungaku-shi, Vol. 8, Kinsei (Tokyo: Iwanami Shoten, 1958), p. 28. The four-part play and five-part play were introduced in 1696 by Ichikawa Danjūrō I. Nishiyama Matsunosuke, Ichikawa Danjūrō (Tokyo: Yoshikawa Kōbunkan, 1960), p. 35.

in a play. Much variation was possible. In fact, as the potential of this multi-part structure was developed, the labels "three-part play," "four-part play," and "five-part play" were kept only to retain a sense of tradition, particularly in the advertisement of productions.[8] They were not literal representations of the actual number of parts in a work, and the word "step" (tate) eventually became the way generally to describe these parts.

The development of the multi-part structure depended on the fact that the basic hanare-kyōgen type of structure was retained; the difference was that this structure was multiplied, or, in other words, "continued." A hanare-kyōgen was a one-part play,[9] and a tsuzuki-kyōgen was a play of two or more parts. This is the same as saying that a tsuzuki-kyōgen was two or more hanare-kyōgen joined together.

The Link Between the Old and New Orders

The multi-part structure was characteristic of both Kamigata and Edo kabuki, but it was the link between the major dramatic sections which distinguished Edo kabuki. The link connected the jidai-mono or "plays of the old order" and the sewa-mono, "plays of the new order." Kabuki was intimately bound up with the social structure of Japan during the Tokugawa period.[10] For the commoners,[11] at whom kabuki was aimed, the old order was that which was established prior to their own emergence as the new order. Since the idea of old order includes social, historical, and artistic elements, the samurai class may be thought of as the old order in relation to the new order of the commoner (in particular, the townsman), and the literature prior to the Tokugawa period as the old order in relation to works

8. This can be seen even today on the traditional-style kabuki billboards (kamban) displayed in front of theaters.
9. Hattori, Kabuki no kōzō, p. 177.
10. The social structure of Japan during the Tokugawa period was represented by a four-tier class hierarchy. Samurai were at the top, followed by the commoners: farmers, artisans, and merchants. Jidai-mono, which came first on a kabuki program, were samurai-related, and sewa-mono, which came second, were commoner-related.
11. The term "commoner" in relation to kabuki mainly refers to the artisans and merchants who lived in the cities where kabuki was performed. Farmers, because they did not live in the cities, did not actively participate in kabuki (either as audience members—except in the summer—or as characters represented in the dramas). Artisans and merchants made up the newly-emergent townsman (chōnin) class of the Tokugawa period.

composed during that period. Of course, as kabuki developed and as the commoner rose in the cultural and economic hierarchy, the new order itself became old.

This linking was the logical final step in the development of the multi-part structure of kabuki. It was in the nature of a transformation: the old order—that which was fixed and idealized—was renewed and regenerated through the new order—that which was newly developed and not yet perfected. As in the case of Sukeroku, the transformation was best accomplished by means of the technique of double identity.

Sekai and Shukō: Tradition and Innovation

Shortly after the start of the farewell production, attention was directed to the next theater year. Work on the new program officially began on the evening of the twelfth day of the ninth month at a meeting called the kao-mise sekai sadame, "deciding the sekai of the kao-mise production." This meeting was the most important point in the theater calendar. It was where a cycle ended and where a new one began. The theater manager, the head actors, and the head playwright gathered to decide the subject matter of the dramas to be performed in the coming year. It was then up to the play-wrights, in conjunction with the actors, to work out the specific treatment of the subject matter.

The crux of kabuki dramatic structure lay in the process represented by the principles of sekai and shukō. The importance of these principles was first made clear in a brief passage called "Matters concerning vertical and horizontal plots" (Tate-suji yoko-suji no koto) found in the Kezairoku (1801), a manual for writers of plays and novels.[12] In effect the earliest attempt to

---

12. Completed in 1801, the Kezairoku was transmitted in manuscript form until 1908, when it was published for the first time. There is some uncertainty about who wrote the Kezairoku; the only clue to the author's identity is the pen name-palindrome, Nyūgatei Ganyū. While it is generally accepted that this is the signature of the minor playwright Namiki Shōzō II (? -1807) and that it was he who is responsible for the work in its present form, it is likely that the contents reflect the teachings of Namiki Shōzō I (1730-73), Nagawa Kamesuke (fl. ca. 1765-90), Namiki Gohei I (1747-1808), and other major playwrights of Shōzō II's day.

The Kezairoku is reprinted in Kinsei geidō-ron, ed. Nishiyama Matsunosuke, et al., Nihon shisō taikei, 61 (Tokyo: Iwanami Shoten, 1972), pp. 493-532. The passage referred to is on pp. 511-12.

define kabuki dramatic structure, it says that the plot of a kabuki play is a product of the interaction of two kinds of plots, the "vertical" and the "horizontal." These represent, respectively, sekai and shukō.

The purpose of sekai, as represented by the vertical plot, was to provide the general outline of a play by using characters and events of familiar works or drama and other forms of fiction. A sekai, which literally means "world," was a kind of tradition or traditional framework within the drama. The role of shukō, as represented by the horizontal plot, was to transform this traditional material into something new. A shukō was an innovation. While the quality of newness is essential to the effectiveness of any kind of drama, the newness of a kabuki play was not so much a departure from past practice as it was a reworking of already established practice. The perfect expression of this is in the traditional calendar, where every year new plays were performed which in subject matter and structure were a continuation of the plays of the past.

But why call sekai the vertical plot and shukō the horizontal plot? It appears that the words vertical and horizontal were used as graphic expressions of dimensions in time, thus making it clear that kabuki had a dual temporal structure. The vertical represented the past in its complete and unchanging form and the horizontal represented the present in its unfolding and ever-changing form. Although the so-called vertical plot gave primary definition to a play, the horizontal plot was needed to bring a work out of the past into the present.

Sekai and shukō represented the dynamics of kabuki dramatic structure. In defining jidai and sewa, which underlie sekai and shukō, as the old order and the new order, the process that took place may be referred to as one of transformation. The old was transformed into the new and the new in turn became old. It was a cycle that might have continued forever.

Sekai: The Use of Traditional Frameworks

The passage from the Kezairoku showed that the concept of sekai was central to kabuki. Its origin as a device in drama, however, was in jōruri.[13] Some have suggested that late in the seventeenth century kabuki playwrights turned to jōruri as a source of material. It was then that works that had been dramatized for jōruri were made into new works for kabuki. In terms of sekai,

13. Shuzui Kenji, Kabuki-geki gikyoku kōzō no kenkyū (Tokyo: Hokuryūkan, 1947), p. 37.

kabuki took over those traditional frameworks that had originally been "made for" jōruri.[14]

It is further suggested that kabuki became derivative of jōruri. Rather than invent completely new characters and situations, after all, kabuki relied instead on those which had already been tried and proven in jōruri. This, however, does not take into account a fundamental feature of the arts in Japan. Japanese dramatic arts, from nō and kōwaka to kabuki and jōruri, are not mutually exclusive, but all have borrowed or have been borrowed from at one time or another. Jōruri playwrights themselves from the beginning used much material that had been developed and dramatized long before the Tokugawa period. Tradition and continuity are essential elements in Japanese aesthetics, and for one art form to use the materials of an older, established one is not only good but also desirable. By so doing, new forms and approaches can be developed, and at the same time a certain cultural cohesiveness is maintained. This is precisely the thought pattern underlying sekai and shukō in kabuki.

On the twelfth day of the ninth month of the year, the managers, head-actors, and head-playwright of the theaters gathered for the kao-mise sekai sadame. Depending on which actors signed contracts with a company, plays with a certain distribution of roles were needed. The function of a sekai was to supply these role requirements by providing the basic plot and character constellation of a play.

In choosing a sekai, the heads of the theaters were aided by works such as the Sekai kōmoku, which was probably compiled in the late eighteenth century.[15] It lists one hundred and fifty sekai, giving the names of the characters in them, as well as the jōruri and literary or historical works which were their sources and to which playwrights could refer for more information.

The most striking feature of the Sekai kōmoku is that it is a rough outline of the history of Japanese literature. The titles of the sekai are works of fiction or the names of characters and events which represent such works.

14. Shuzui, Kinsei gikyoku kenkyū (Tokyo: Chūkōkan, 1932), p. 33.
15. The authorship of the Sekai kōmoku is uncertain, but like the Kezairoku several playwrights probably contributed to it. It was most recently reprinted in Kyōgen sakusha shiryō-shū (1): Sekai kōmoku, shibai nenjū-gyōji, pp. 7-84.
     See also the section entitled "Sekai kōmoku no seiritsu nendai" in the article "Naimaze to sekai" by Urayama Masao in Geinō no kagaku, Vol. 5 of Geinō ronkō II, ed. Tokyo Kokuritsu Bunkazai Kenkyūjo Geinōbu (Tokyo: Heibonsha, 1974), pp. 103-20.

The works of fiction cover a wide spectrum beginning with the earliest myths and legends, such as those found in the Kojiki (712) and Nihon shoki (720), and extending to works of jōruri and kabuki in the Tokugawa period. While it is true that the Sekai kōmoku drew on many of the most famous works in the history of Japanese literature, it was not comprehensive. Only materials which had already been dramatized, mainly in the form of nō, kōwaka, jōruri, and kabuki were included.

Iizuka Tomoichirō has pointed out that by the last decades of the Tokugawa period choosing the sekai for the kao-mise production had changed from a true discussion meeting to a merely perfunctory and ceremonial affair.[16] The reason was that in time kabuki became classicized, as is shown by the contents of the Sekai kōmoku itself. The Sekai kōmoku analyzed the entire contemporary repertory of kabuki according to traditional frameworks, and is a predecessor of Iizuka's own Kabuki saiken (1926).[17]

The Kabuki saiken is essentially an updated version of the Sekai kōmoku. By comparing the number of entries in each work it is easy to see that sekai and shukō did indeed represent a process in which new material was constantly added to the kabuki repertory. Whereas the Sekai kōmoku lists one hundred and fifty sekai, the Kabuki saiken, published over a century later, contains two hundred and seventy-five.

How are the entries in the Sekai kōmoku classified? Not surprisingly, they are mainly divided into jidai and sewa. There was some ambiguity about how to categorize plays based on struggles for power within the houses of feudal lords (ō-ie kyōgen). Although these plays concerned the samurai class, the stories of rivalries were timely subjects in the Tokugawa period and therefore fall between jidai and sewa. Another problematic category was religious plays, whose timeless quality made it difficult to classify as either jidai or sewa.[18]

In the entry for each sekai were names of its characters and titles of related works. The Gikeiki sekai is typical. It contains the names of forty-six characters, including Yoshitsune, Benkei, and Tadanobu, with the note that there are many more and that the reader should consult listings under the Heike monogatari and Izu nikki, among others, for more of them. The entry also contains the names of characters from that part of the Gikeiki that

16. Iizuka Tomoichirō, Kabuki gairon (Tokyo: Hakubunkan, 1928), pp. 495-97.
17. Iizuka, Kabuki saiken (Tokyo: Daiichi Shobō, 1927).
18. Urayama, "Naimaze to sekai," pp. 108-110.

concerns Jōruri Gozen (Princess Jōruri), which by itself forms a small sub-sekai. Following the characters there is a list of sources for the Gikeiki sekai. The Azuma kagami (ca. 1270), which is the historical chronicle of the Kamakura bakufu, is an example. This in turn is followed by a list of approximately thirty jōruri titles in the sekai, ranging from the very familiar Yoshitsune sembon-zakara to the less familiar Tadanobu migawari monogatari and Kumasaka monogatari. This pattern of giving the names of characters, literary or historical sources or both, and jōruri works is followed to a greater or lesser degree in each entry.

Each traditional framework of course was not equal in importance to every other—importance being determined by how frequently a framework was used in the construction of kabuki plays. Among all the sekai that are listed three stand out as being used far more than any of the others. These are the Gikeiki, Soga, and to a slightly lesser degree, the Heike sekai.[19]

The importance of these three works is related in an interesting way to issues concerning Japanese literature in general. In her article, "Medieval Jongleurs and the Making of a National Literature," Barbara Ruch argues that the Muromachi period saw the development of a national literature, which she defines as:

> a certain core of literary works the content of which is well known and held dear by the majority of people across all class and professional lines, a literature that is a reflection of a national outlook. Such literature never shocks or revolutionizes; it is constituted of favorite themes that recur again and again of which people never tire. . . . This national literature may, indeed must, cross genre lines.[20]

She points out that as a result of the development of this national literature "for the first time Japan . . . came to share one body of heroes and heroines."[21] And the three "works" she cites as examples of such a literature

19. According to Atsumi, "Sekai to tōjō-jimbutsu," in Kabuki zensho, ed. Toita Yasuji (Tokyo: Sōgensha, 1956), II, p. 78, the Soga sekai has the greatest number of plays associated with it.
20. Barbara Ruch, "Medieval Jongleurs and the Making of a National Literature," in Japan in the Muromachi Age, ed. John Whitney Hall and Toyoda Takeshi (Berkeley: University of California Press, 1977), pp. 291-92.
21. Ibid., p. 293.

are, not unexpectedly, the Gikeiki, Soga monogatari, and Heike monogatari.[22] The sekai of kabuki are, in fact, part of this national literature. That Ruch has identified such a phenomenon from a perspective different from that of kabuki underscores its importance in Japanese literature as a whole.

The relationship between sekai and shukō was not static; it worked precisely because it was not. Time was the crucial element. Shuzui Kenji has shown that what are considered traditional frameworks differ depending on the historical period under consideration.[23] For a work of fiction to be a sekai, it had to be sanctioned by repeated dramatization over time. It was then familiar to audiences and became, essentially, a frame of reference that the playwright could presume the audience possessed. By the time the Sekai kōmoku was compiled a considerable number of such frames were already available. Of course, not all of the items listed in the Sekai kōmoku were always sekai. Sekai of sewa plays in particular needed time to develop and to gain a permanent place in the repertory. To give an example of the importance of time in the making of sekai, in the third month of 1708 the story of Yaoya Oshichi (the lady who burned down Edo so she could be near her lover) was used as a shukō in the play based on the sekai of Chūjō Hime (a very devout Buddhist princess of ancient times). The play was Chūjō Hime Kyō-hina, performed at the Nakamura-za. In time the story of Yaoya Oshichi gained the status of a sekai and was included in the Sekai kōmoku.[24]

Taking Gunji's analogy one step further, we may say that traditional frameworks are idealizations (omo-tadashii-mono), in contrast to which shukō work as counterpoints (modoki). This means, of course, that by the end of the eighteenth century, when the Sekai kōmoku was compiled, both plays classified as jidai and those classified as sewa were idealizations. And this was exactly the case. Around that time the kabuki repertory ceased to grow, in effect becoming entirely traditional. One way to renew the traditional material was to combine two or more sekai in a single work.

22. Ibid., p. 292.
23. Shuzui, Kabuki-geki gikyoku kōzō no kenkyū, pp. 36-37.
24. Okazaki Yoshie refers to innovations as being "fragmentary" (dampen-teki) at first and gives the Yaoya Oshichi shukō in the Chūjō Hime sekai as a particular example. Okazaki Yoshie, "Genroku kabuki no sekai kōzō," in his Nihon bungeigaku (Tokyo: Iwanami Shoten, 1935), p. 336.

Traditional Frameworks and the Law

Playwrights could use traditional frameworks to circumvent certain restrictions imposed by the government on theatrical presentations. The government had stipulated "that matter concerning (itself) must not be published, that the names of contemporary members of the samurai class and above must not be mentioned, nor any incidents involving samurai occuring after 1600."[25] These orders were issed before 1700, but in 1703 when the incident of the forty-seven masterless samurai was first dramatized, it was further decreed that "unusual events of the times or action resembling them must not be acted out."[26] These laws were actually bans on direct representation, rather than on representation itself, which could be accomplished in other ways. Taking the case of the forty-seven samurai as an example, even though direct representation of the character Asano of Akō was not permitted, it was acceptable to have En'ya Hangan from the Taiheiki sekai substituted for him.[27] Putting what was to become popularly known as Chūshingura into the framework of the Taiheiki was quite different from giving all the characters fictitious names. By using the Taiheiki, it simply appeared that the theater was putting on another Taiheiki play which, of course, had the sanction of long use and, at any rate, concerned events before 1600.

Using the framework of the Taiheiki in this way was in itself dramatically effective. Audiences were familiar with the work and could easily make the mental leap from Taiheiki to Chūshingura. The play as we know it today contains anachronisms, such as references to samisens and gay quarters, which did not exist at the time of the Taiheiki. These directly underscore the fact that the play was not just about those characters and events of the Taiheiki. Even in the West some playwrights have found this type of indirect representation more desirable than direct representation, especially when speaking of current events that are particularly shocking to the community. One is especially reminded of Arthur Miller's The Crucible, where Miller used the framework of the Salem witch trials to write about

25. Donald H. Shively, "Bakufu versus Kabuki," Harvard Journal of Asiatic Studies, 18 (1955), 351.
26. Ibid., 352.
27. On the same page cited in note 26 above, Shively mentions some of the conventions associated with name substitution.
    The incident of the forty-seven masterless samurai was first dramatized as part of the Soga sekai, but it was banned immediately. See Chūshingura (The Treasury of Loyal Retainers), translated by Donald Keene (New York: Columbia University Press, 1971), pp. 3-4.

McCarthyism in the 1950s, and similarly Jean Anouilh's Antigone, where he used a framework from ancient Greek drama to write about Nazism. In Western drama such examples are relatively isolated ones in comparison with kabuki, which was a dramatic form whose foundation lay in the use of traditional frameworks.

Shukō: Three Types of Innovation

Compared with sekai, shukō were, of course far less fixed. While traditional frameworks may be labeled and compiled in a work like the Sekai kōmoku, it is difficult to do the same in the case of innovations. This is because the principle of innovation necessarily implies a state of constant change. Though innovations could in time become traditional frameworks, they started out as counterpoints to existing ones.

Shukō is an important principle in Japanese aesthetics in general but it acquired particular importance in the Tokugawa period, especially in the new arts of haikai, ukiyo-e, and kabuki, each of which was an art of innovation.[28] It may even be said that innovation is the defining element of Tokugawa literature.[29]

Innovation makes something new out of something old. As the Kezairoku suggests, in kabuki sekai are old. It then follows that to understand shukō, it is necessary to analyze the three ways in which they made sekai new.

The first encompasses those changes that were made within a traditional framework and employs the technique of kakikae, or the rewriting of plays. Shibaraku and Taimen are two excellent examples. Although both works may be regarded as part of larger frameworks, each possesses its own character constellation and plot outline. Shibaraku was performed in the eleventh month every year and Taimen in the first month. And every year these plays were rewritten. While keeping the same basic framework certain changes in character and situation were made. This type of innovation features a lack of fixed texts—even though a play may have been produced many times. Only since the Meiji era have such plays as Shibaraku and Taimen acquired set texts.

---

28. Gunji, Kabuki no bigaku (Tokyo: Engeki Shuppansha, 1975), p. 74.
29. Nakamura Yukihiko, "Modes of Expression in a Historical Context," Acta Asiatica, 28 (1975), 8-10.

The second type of innovation is when a play that was previously unknown or unused in kabuki was added to a sekai, as Sukeroku was to a Soga play. It was usual in this case for the new work to be a sewa-mono and for it to be joined to a jidai-mono. The joining was done by means of a transformation of character, accomplished by the technique of double identity.[30] Besides Sukeroku, other innovations that were added to the Soga sekai in the same way were the stories of Ume no Yoshibei, Ososme and Hisamatsu, and Sankatsu and Hanshichi.[31]

The third type of innovation occurs when two or more sekai are joined. This is commonly called naimaze (which literally means to twist—as in making a rope--and to mix). Naimaze is often confused with the second type of innovation. Although naimaze simply means putting two or more sekai together, it is often thought of as equal to the joining of a jidai- and sewa-mono. Though this certainly underlies the principles of sekai and shukō in general, it is not naimaze. As Urayama Masao has shown, the different sekai do not retain their separate natures as such but are brought together to form an entirely new work.[32]

Naimaze was the last type of innovation to develop, and it marked the end of kabuki's growth as a dramatic art form. The technique began to be employed near the end of the eighteenth century, when kabuki was already starting to look upon itself as a classic form. This move toward classicism is reflected in the formulation of the jūhachi-ban, the writing of the Kezairoku, the compilation of the Sekai kōmoku, and in the publication of kabuki texts. Naimaze was a popular technique for several decades, especially as used by the playwrights Tsuruya Namboku IV (1755-1829) and Kawatake Mokuami (1816-1893)--who is considered to be the last major playwright of kabuki.

30. This second type of innovation is sometimes referred to in Japanese as yatsushi, "disguising."
31. Urayama, "Naimaze to sekai," p. 107.
32. Ibid.

PART TWO: SUKEROKU'S DOUBLE IDENTITY

Chapter III

SUKEROKU AS SOGA GORŌ, A GOD-HERO OF THE NATION: THE DEVELOPMENT OF THE SOGA TRADITION

In analyzing the significance of Sukeroku's double identity, the first step is to elucidate the symbolism of the character Soga Gorō as portrayed by Ichikawa Danjūrō I (1660-1704), the great actor and playwright who was in many ways the father of Edo kabuki. This will be done by tracing the evolution of the Soga tradition from its origins in nō, kōwaka, and ko-jōruri to its appearance in the Edo kabuki. Nō and kōwaka are dramatic forms that began before the Tokugawa period. Ko-jōruri, or "old" jōruri, flourished during the early Tokugawa period.

This historical approach is best because kabuki was based on the long-term accumulation of characters and themes, many of which antedated the birth of kabuki. Danjūrō's portrayal of Soga Gorō in Edo kabuki depended on Gorō's having been established as a central figure among the dramatis personae of earlier dramatic forms. Representations of Soga Gorō before Danjūrō I established the character in the minds of audiences as a strong and awesome being. Danjūrō's great achievement was to use the tradition that had built up around Gorō in combination with acting techniques inspired by Kimpira jōruri (a short-lived and very violent form of seventeenth-century Edo puppet and recitative theater). In so doing he created the aragoto or "rough" style of Edo kabuki and brought Gorō to the highest possible level in the hierarchy of dramatic characterization: as a living god-hero for the people of Edo.

The Soga Brothers' Revenge

The Soga brothers' revenge is one of the most popular and enduring stories in Japan. Supposedly based on an actual event which occurred during the Kamakura period, it is an heroic tale of how two brothers, Soga no Jūrō

Sukenari and Soga no Gorō Tokimune, devoted their young lives to avenging the murder of their father. The devotion that enabled them to endure eighteen difficult years of waiting before they were finally able to carry out the revenge, and the fact that the revenge cost them their own lives, have combined to make the brothers ideal examples of filial piety and samurai honor.

The enemy of the brothers was Kudō Suketsune. Angered at the father of Kawazu no Saburō Sukeshige over a matter involving what he believed to be his rightful inheritance, he had Sukeshige killed. Sukeshige was his own cousin and the father of the Soga brothers, who were small children at the time. Even though Suketsune's dispute with Sukeshige's father was not unjust, his resolution of the problem was. And the only thing the brothers could think of as they were growing up was revenge—to console their mother and to restore family honor.

The revenge was finally carried out on the twenty-eighth day of the fifth month of 1193, eighteen years after Sukeshige was killed. After several unsuccessful attempts, Jūrō and Gorō trapped Suketsune at a hunt arranged by Minamoto no Yoritomo (1147-1199), the de facto ruler of Japan at that time, at the foot of Mt. Fuji. Jūrō was killed in the ensuing fight that broke out with Suketsune's retainers. Gorō escaped, but was eventually captured. He was forced to die even though Yoritomo admired his bravery. In accordance with traditional practice in cases of outstanding acts of heroism and sacrifice, Yoritomo ordered temples erected and prayers said for the Soga brothers.

The popularity of the Soga brothers' story was the product of its characters, themes, and geographical appeal. The leading characters were, of course, the brothers themselves. With their contrasting natures—Jūrō tended to be cool and calm while Gorō was hot-blooded and quick to act—which became more pronounced the more the story was told and dramatized, the brothers stood for a kind of heroic Japanese Everyman. In Japan the traditional view of human nature is that it is made up of two sides, one calm and one violent, which balance each other.[1] The two brothers perfectly represented these two sides.

---

1. As Anesaki Masaharu put it, "The soul was believed to be composed of two parts, one mild, refined, and happy, the other rough, brutal, and raging (the mild, nigi-mitama, and the rough, ara-mitama). The former cares for its possessor's health and prosperity, while the latter performs adventurous tasks or even malicious deeds." Anesaki, History of Japanese Religion (London: Kegan Paul, Trench, Trubner, 1930), p. 40.

The story's theme of vendetta was an important one in Japanese thought and literature. Japanese society placed high value on "face" and honor, and revenge was a necessary course of action when the scales of honor were somehow unbalanced.[2] In contrast to the vendetta in Chūshingura, which was carried out by almost fifty samurai, the Soga brothers' revenge was accomplished with very little help. This of course put even more emphasis on the phenomenal and heroic determination of Jūrō and Gorō.

The character of the brothers and their vendetta had universal interest, but the story's setting in the eastern part of Japan gave it special geographical appeal—particularly in the Tokugawa period when Edo was the capital of the shōgun and a city of samurai. Soga plays were performed in Kamigata kabuki, but they never occupied the position of importance they did in Edo.[3]

The Soga monogatari, literally "Soga Tale," is the representative written work of the Soga brothers' revenge. It began as a work recited by storytellers. Some of them were goze[4] (blind women) who told—possibly chanted or sang—the tale, accompanying themselves by beating on a drum.[5]

2. Okakura Yoshisaburō found a connection between revenge and Japanese love of purity:
> Many of the so-called mental peculiarities of the Japanese owe their origin to the love of purity and its complementary hatred of defilement. But, pray, how could it be otherwise, being trained, as we actually are, to look upon slights inflicted, either on our family honor or on the national pride, as so many defilements and wounds that would not be clean and heal up again, unless by a thorough washing through vindication? You may consider the cases of vendetta so often met with in the public and private life of Japan, merely as a kind of morning tub which a people take with whom love of cleanliness has grown into a passion.

Quoted by Ruth Benedict in The Chrysanthemum and the Sword (Boston: Houghton Mifflin, 1946), pp. 161–62.
3. Soga plays were performed in Kamigata kabuki by the great actor Sakata Tōjūrō (1647–1709). See Gunji, Namari to suigin, p. 16. Unlike Ichikawa Danjūrō I, Tōjūrō did not have a male heir or capable pupil to contine his work, which may be one reason why Soga plays lost popularity in the Kamigata area after Tōjūrō died.
4. Ruch, "Medieval Joungleurs and the Making of a National Literature," p. 295.
5. Soga monogatari, in Ichiko Teiji and Ōshima Tatehiko (eds.), Nihon koten bungaku taikei, 88 (Tokyo: Iwanami Shoten, 1966), pp. 5–6. Among the original sources of the information are Shichi-jū-ichi-ban uta-awase (dating from the early 1500s) and the nō play Mochizuki, in which a woman becomes a blind storyteller and tells how Ichiman Hakoō (Soga Gorō) avenged his father's murder.

In time the story developed a well-established character constellation and general plot outline--in short, a tradition--that could be used over and over again as suited the art and purposes of different storytellers.

Once the tradition had been created, the storyteller, in order to satisfy the audience's desire for something new and different, found it necessary to invent episodes and fit them into the familiar framework. In turn, these inventions, if they could survive the test of time, crystallized and became part of the tradition; other innovations could be made in counterpoint to them. In the case of the Soga tradition, the storyteller was just one of the "performers" of the story, as in a more literal sense were the players of nō and kōwaka, and later those of ko-jōruri, jōruri, and kabuki.

The question of how the written text fits into this performance process is an interesting one, although beyond the scope of this book. Suffice it to say, however, that after the story had been developed to a degree as an oral tale, it was written down, probably by a monk, using a kind of modified Chinese (hentai kambun) writing system.[6] This first Soga monogatari dates from the Muromachi period and is in ten volumes. Later written versions differed more in writing systems than in actual contents--until the twelve volume rufu-bon (popular edition) was published in the Tokugawa period.[7] The rufu-bon has two more volumes than previous texts because it contains a number of incidents not found in the earlier editions. These incidents are by and large the innovations that had become part of the Soga traditional framework through their dramatization in nō and particularly in kōwaka.[8] The Soga tradition was developed in the course of dramatic performance, and this is reflected in the textual development of the Soga monogatari.[9]

---

6. Soga monogatari, p. 7.
7. Among the various editions, the rufu-bon is of most interest both to students of drama and to readers in general. See Gunji, "Soga monogatari to Soga kyōgen," Engeki-kai, 8, No. 2 (1950), 5.
  With the birth of the publishing trade in the early seventeenth century, the Soga monogatari became a best-seller in its rufu-bon edition. By the Genroku period, it had gone through at least six printings. The earliest known one was in the Kan'ei era (1624-41). Its popularity is testified to in an anecdote which relates that even courtesans kept copies of it in the toko-no-ma of their rooms. See Ibid.
8. The relationship between kōwaka--as preserved in mai no hon texts--and the texts of the Soga monogatari has been of interest to scholars. It has been said that kōwaka are the link between the shinji-bon and rufu-bon versions and are perhaps, in fact, the direct source of the rufu-bon. Muroki Yatarō, Katarimono (mai, sekkyō, ko-jōruri) no kenkyū (Tokyo: Kazama Shobō, 1970), p. 163.

Moreover, Yanagita Kunio hypothesized that the characters Tora Gozen and Tora no Shōshō, the lovers of Jūrō and Gorō, were actually introduced by the goze who first told the Soga story. Whether this is true or not is difficult to prove, but it does at least suggest one possible kind of connection between performances of the story and its textual development.[10]

The Origins of the Soga Tradition
In Nō, Kōwaka, and Ko-jōruri

The first entry in the Kabuki nempyō suggests that Soga plays, along with those based on the Gikeiki (the story of the hero Yoshitsune), were already popular and being performed early in the history of kabuki. The entry is for the year 1559 and says that "Okuni and others performed (plays based on) the Gikeiki and the Soga Revenge for the Shōgun (Ashikaga) Yoshiteru."[11] Although the information is clearly anachronistic (Okuni is usually thought to have first performed kabuki some forty years later), it does point out that kabuki depended on established traditional frameworks, especially those of the Soga monogatari and Gikeiki.

How were Soga and other traditions that became popular in kabuki established even before Okuni did her first play? They were formulated in the repertories of other dramatic forms. Before discussing the Soga tradition in relation to Danjūrō I, it is necessary first to look at it as it had developed up to his time, in nō, kōwaka, and ko-jōruri.[12] Brief summaries of plays and repertories, such as those given below, cannot do justice to the evolution of a

9. See Kobayashi Shizuo, "Soga monogatari to kusemai," Koten kenkyū, 6, No. 4 (1941), 96-101, and Sakamoto Setchō, "Soga monogatari to yōkyoku," Nōgaku, 2, No. 6 (1951), 2-12, and No. 7, 2-13.
10. Soga monogatari, p. 10. For more information on Shōshō and Tora Gozen as storytellers, see Gunji, "Soga monogatari to Soga kyōgen," 5. This also suggests a possible source of the erotic, "womanly" innovations in the Soga sekai. See Ruch, "Medieval Jongleurs and the Making of a National Literature," p. 301.
11. Ihara, Kabuki nempyō, I, p. 3. Yoshiteru (1536-65) was the thirteenth Ashikaga shōgun.
The original source of the information is the Kabuki jishi, reprinted in Kabuki, Vol. 6 of Nihon shomin bunka shiryō shūsei, 87-133, relevant passage on pp. 93-94. The Kabuki jishi is an interesting, though unfortunately not wholly reliable, work on various aspects of kabuki history and performance. It was written by Tamenaga Itchō and published in 1762.
12. Before the time of Danjūrō I, the only dramatic art forms to treat the Soga sekai in an important way were nō, kōwaka, and ko-jōruri.

major dramatic tradition, but they will at least give some idea of the nature of the material on which Danjūrō built his Soga dramatizations.

The Soga Tradition in Nō and Kōwaka

Among the approximately two hundred and forty works in the current nō repertory, there are five Soga plays: Chōbuku Soga, Gembuku Soga, Ko-sode Soga, Yo-uchi Soga, and Zenji Soga. In the total known repertory of more than two thousand titles, there are perhaps ten additional Soga works that are no longer performed—or perhaps never were performed.[13] Among the fifty surviving texts of kōwaka (the mai no hon) seven are Soga plays. These are Ichiman Hakoō, Gempuku Soga (note: in nō the title is Gembuku, in kōwaka it is Gempuku), Wada sakamori, Ko-sode Soga, Tsurugi sandan, Yo-uchi Soga, and Jūbangiri.[14]

The authorship and dates of composition of the Soga plays of both nō and kōwaka are not known with certainty. In the case of nō, however, it is thought that Miyamasu may have composed the five works that are extant.[15] Very little is known about Miyamasu. He is thought to have lived slightly later than the playwrights Motomasa (ca. 1394–1432) and Zenchiku (1405–ca. 1470) and to have toured the eastern provinces of Japan as a member of a sarugaku troupe.[16] In the eastern provinces, where the Soga story was set, Miyamasu may have transformed the already popular tale into the nō form.

Among the five works, Chōbuku Soga[17] is not only the most distinctive, but it is also related in the most interesting way to Danjūrō I's kabuki Soga plays. It is the earliest Taimen play, that is, a work treating of the first confrontation between the Soga brothers and their enemy Kudō Suketsune. In this case, however, the encounter does not involve Jūrō; it is only between Gorō and Suketsune. In fact, in Chōbuku Soga, Gorō is not yet Gorō; he is still

13. Plays for which there is no record of performance may have been used only for chanting purposes, according to Tanaka Makoto. Moreover, it is difficult to determine the number of Soga plays of nō using only the titles of plays because some plays with different titles had the same contents. See Tanaka, "Yōkyoku no haikyoku," in Nogami Toyoichirō (ed.), Nōgaku zensho (Tokyo: Sōgensha, 1942), III, 337–80.
14. See James T. Araki, The Ballad Drama of Medieval Japan (Berkeley: University of California Press, 1964), pp. 133–39.
15. Tanaka, "Soga-mono yōkyoku ni tsuite," Hōsei, 19, No. 11 (1943), 73.
16. Gondō, Nō no mikata, p. 52.
17. Chōbuku Soga has been translated by Laurence Bresler in Monumenta Nipponica, 29, No. 1 (1974), 69–81.

a child named Hakoō living in the Hakone temple where his mother left him to train for the priesthood so that he could devote his life to praying for his father's soul. As everyone knows, however, Hakoō is not destined to become a priest. He will leave the temple in order to carry out the revenge.

The crux of the play lies in the contrast between a terribly strong-willed, but as yet powerless, boy and his seemingly unassailable enemy, who arrives at the Hakone temple one day as a samurai retainer in the entourage of no less a figure of power and authority than Yoritomo. Because of the tremendous frustration that Hakoō experiences in this momentous meeting, the priest of the temple performs a chōbuku (curse) for him, the outcome of which is the highly symbolic appearance of the guardian deity Fudō Myōō who assures all watching that one day the revenge will indeed be done.

Chōbuku Soga is in two parts. It opens with the arrival of Kudō Suketsune and Minamoto no Yoritomo at the temple in the Hakone mountains. They meet the chief priest of the temple and Hakoō. The latter questions the priest about the identity of the visitors, only to learn that Kudō Suketsune (whom Hakoō had never seen before) is among those accompanying Yoritomo. Suketsune audaciously addresses Hakoō on the subject of his father Sukeshige's death, though he has no idea of the powerful emotions that he is stirring up in the boy. Hakoō is ready to carry out revenge on the spot, but the priest holds him back.

In the second part of the play Fudō appears. According to popular belief, Fudō Myōō is a Buddha who has been changed into a being of terrible and frightening appearance in order to act as a guardian of men in a world filled with evil spirits.

> Though never so horrendous in appearance as the Tibetan angry deities, the face of Fudo is nevertheless startling. . . . One eye glares downwards, the other squints divergently upwards. With one upper tooth grasping his upper lip, his mouth is twisted into a peculiar snarl. His long hair hangs in a coil over his left shoulder. His right hand grasps a sword and his left a rope, and he stands not on a lotus or an animal mount as do many Buddhist divinities, but on an immovable rock, which rises sometimes from curling waves. Always he is ringed round with fire.[18]

---

18. Carmen Blacker, The Catalpa Bow: A Study of Shamanistic Practices in Japan (London: George Allen and Unwin, 1975), p. 175.

The climax of Chōbuku Soga comes when Fudō destroys an effigy (katashiro) of Suketsune and brings the play to a close with the words: "In the end, (by the power of this curse) Hakoō will succeed (in avenging his father's murder)."

The play is a masterpiece of irony and contrast. Great forces gather amidst the serenity of a mountain temple. Suketsune believes that the boy Hakoō cannot do him any harm, but in the end he will be proved wrong. The point is brilliantly underscored when Suketsune is "transformed" (theatrically, by using the same actor--the shite) into Fudō, who, as we have seen, makes certain of Suketsune's ultimate destruction.

At the same time, Hakoō is also metaphorically transformed into Fudō. After all, neither Suketsune nor Hakoō appear as such in the second part of the play. As the audience knew, Hakoō must wait for a long time to carry out his revenge, and it is his spirit of resolve through those long years that makes him such a tremendous and even superhuman figure in the Soga sekai. In a broad sense, Hakoō as Fudō represents a determination to rid the world of the all too powerful and therefore evil forces (represented by Suketsune) that would overwhelm the less powerful forces (represented by Hakoō), and to restore the world to its proper balance. Danjūrō I's use of the Soga sekai, and his interpretation of Soga Gorō in particular, came close to a Gorō manifested as Fudō. In fact, Danjūrō consciously adopted Fudō as the symbolic model of his aragoto art.[19]

The other four Soga nō plays, while important, do not have quite the same power as Chōbuku Soga. Gembuku Soga concerns Hakoō's leaving the Hakone temple and undergoing the coming-of-age rites (gembuku) so that he may finally carry out his revenge as a man. In the play Jūrō goes to Hakone to take Hakoō from the temple, but before Hakoō can be released, Jūrō must get permission from the head priest. Although it means going against their mother's wishes--eventually leading her to disown Hakoō--the priest, who is sympathetic to the brothers' cause, allows Hakoō to go. When the brothers set out, he comes after them with a long sword to present to Hakoō in honor of his coming of age, the ceremony of which has been performed by Jūrō on the road. It is this sword, which is said to be a gift from Yoshitsune, that figures so centrally in Sukeroku.

Ko-sode Soga contains the reconciliation of Gorō and his mother, which is also the farewell meeting of mother and sons before the revenge is carried

19. See Nishiyama, Ichikawa Danjūrō, pp. 17-18.

out. As a result of the action depicted in Gembuku Soga (namely, leaving the temple where the mother had intended her younger son remain), Hakoō (now Gorō) had been disowned. a reconciliation takes place, and although Jūrō and Gorō rejoice, expressing their happiness in music and dance (which are the focus of the play), this is soon supplanted by lamentation at the thought of imminent separation from their mother.

Yo-uchi Soga[20] concerns the revenge itself. The strength of the play lies in the emotional contrast between the necessity of carrying out the revenge in order to restore family honor and the strong attachment of Gorō and Jūrō to their mother and their two retainers, Oniō and Dōzaburō, who are prepared to (but do not) join their masters in death.

The story of Zenji Soga, the last play of the five, opens with Oniō and Dōzaburō's visit to the Soga mother to bring her some of her sons' personal effects to keep as mementos. While lamenting the deaths of Gorō and Jūrō, she is at the same time concerned about the safety of her surviving son, Kugami no Zenji. He is at Kugami Temple, where she sends Oniō and Dōzaburō to look after him, but before they can get there he has been captured and sent off to Kamakura on the orders of Yoritomo. This can only upset the balance that had been restored when Gorō and Jūrō carried out their revenge on Suketsune, and contributes to the belief that that Soga brothers' struggle continued even after they were dead.

Unlike nō, which is well known and performed by amateurs and professionals alike throughout Japan, kōwaka is not well known and survives today only in the Village of Ōe in Fukuoka Prefecture (Kyūshū). It has been performed there for the past four centuries, since late in the sixteenth century, when a kōwaka master came to teach the art to the samurai retainers of Kamachi Hyōgo-no-kami Akimune, lord of a castle town near present-day Ōe.[21]

While the traditions of kōwaka continued to be transmitted faithfully from generation to generation in the outlying district of Ōe, during the Tokugawa period kōwaka was dying in Edo. There, kōwaka masters enjoyed the prestige of samurai status and seemed to have spent much energy trying to dissociate themselves from the class of entertainers by ridding their performance of its dance elements, and reducing it finally to "simply singing

20. Yo-uchi Soga has been translated by Laurence Kominz in Monumenta Nipponica, 33, No. 4 (1978), 441-59.
21. Araki, The Ballad Drama of Medieval Japan, p. 80.

to a beat produced by the slapping of a fan." These are the words of Takizawa Bakin, a noted writer of the nineteenth century, who also observed in the same entry of Nimaze no ki (1811) that kōwaka—with the dance intact—still survived in Ōe village, "although most people of Edo do not know it."[22]

The survival of kōwaka remained practically a secret until almost a century after Nimaze no ki was written, when Takano Tatsuyuki, a scholar who died in 1948, read the entry and went to Ōe (in 1907) to see if the art of kōwaka had indeed survived there. What he saw in the performances, as well as in the historical and genealogical records of the performers, was the subject of many of his pioneering studies.[23]

Takano's research must have been stimulated also by the reprinting in 1900 of Mai no hon, which James Araki in The Ballad Drama of Medieval Japan translates as "Texts for Kōwaka Dances," and describes as "an anthology of thirty-six standard kōwaka compiled in the early seventeenth century and published as prose tales to be enjoyed in reading."[24] Ueda Kazutoshi, editor of this work, said in the preface that kōwaka, which had long since become a virtually forgotten dramatic art form, was "the equal of the nō drama in its importance to the culture of medieval Japan."[25]

An indication of the importance of kōwaka is that its material was based on two major works of pre-Tokugawa Japan, the Heike monogatari and the Soga monogatari. Kōwaka helped popularize and establish the traditions of these works. Kōwaka are "lively tales which extol the virtuous warrior, exalt valorous and honorable death, and find pleasurable charm in the pathos of tragedy. Loyalty, filial piety, faithfulness, courage, and chivalry are glorified."[26] They are significant precursors of kabuki.

Summaries of the seven Soga works of kōwaka are included in Araki's book.[27] In the matter of story line, the similarities between nō and kōwaka Soga plays can be readily seen. Differences are found mainly in what I call the "distribution" of the story. The kōwaka Gempuku Soga, for example, contains Hakoō's meeting with Kudō Suketsune at the Hakone temple. This, as

22. Nimaze no ki is translated by Araki as "Potpourri of Records." The relevant passage is found on Ibid., p. 6.
23. See, for example, Takano Tatsuyuki, Nihon engeki-shi (Tokyo: Tōkyōdō, 1948), Vol. 2, pp. 89-132.
24. Araki, The Ballad Drama of Medieval Japan, p. 4.
25. Ibid.
26. Ibid., p. 13.
27. Ibid., pp. 136-39.

we have seen, was treated in the nō Chōbuku Soga, which, in my view, makes more effective use of the meeting between Hakoō and Suketsune, and Hakoō's subsequent frustration. Another example of a difference in "distribution" is found in Tsugari sandan. In kōwaka this contains the episode where the priest gave Gorō and Jurō a sword which has special value. In nō this episode is found in Gembuku Soga.

Yet another example of such a difference is found in the nō and kōwaka Yo-uchi Soga. Whereas the nō version contains the scene of the revenge on Suketsune and ends with Jurō's death and Gorō's capture, the kōwaka version stops just before the revenge is executed, the action climaxing at the point where it becomes possible to carry it out. The revenge itself, the ensuing fight between the brothers and Suketsune's retainers, Jurō's death and Gorō's capture are then covered in the kōwaka Jūban-giri. Soga plays of kabuki generally stop before the actual carrying out of the revenge.

Just as Chōbuku Soga is of special interest among the Soga plays of nō, so too is Wada sakamori outstanding among those of kōwaka. And like Chōbuku Soga, Wada sakamori displays an interesting relationship with Danjūrō's Soga works.

The story of Wada sakamori is about Jurō's farewell to his lady-love, the courtesan Oiso no Tora (elsewhere referred to as Tora Gozen). Arriving at her house, he encounters Wada Yoshimori, who had previously helped the brothers in an unsuccessful attempt to carry out the revenge. Friendship notwithstanding, Yoshimori and Jurō are ready to quarrel over the lady. Gorō, whose brotherly instincts tell him that Jurō is about to need his help, arrives at the scene. (He had been at home sharpening arrowheads in preparation for the revenge.[28]) Gorō is poised outside the sliding paper door of the room his brother is in, and just as he is about to attack, Yoshimori's son, the strongman Yoshihide (who, as Asahina, comes to play a major role in the kabuki Soga plays) sees Gorō's image through the door. Yoshihide lunges at Gorō and tries to drag him by his armor into the room. But Yoshihide, for all his strength, cannot budge Gorō. The part of the armor that he was pulling at finally gives way and he tumbles backward into the room. The episode ends with Gorō having the situation well in hand.

The importance of Wada sakamori is that it is the first play in which Gorō is clearly established as a being of great, even superhuman, strength. This scene of his encounter with Yoshihide is reminiscent of Yoshitsune's

28. This scene is the forerunner of the play Ya no ne Gorō.

famous encounter with Benkei on the bridge. Although Yoshitsune and Gorō are in other respects quite different, in both cases a youth encounters someone whose strength is legendary. In this Gorō-Yoshihide encounter, we see the beginnings of the style that gave rise to Danjūrō's aragoto art.[29]

The basic character constellation and plot outlines that were used in later Soga dramatizations were established in nō and kōwaka. The main characters are Soga Gorō and his brother Jūrō, their mother, their two loyal retainers Oniō and Dōzaburō, the courtesan Oiso no Tora, and finally, Kudō Suketsune.[30] The plot revolves around preparations for the revenge, carrying it out, and to a degree, what happened after the deed was done. The focus of the story is the conflict between the larger forces of the state, as represented somewhat abstractly and distantly by Yoritomo, and personally and closely by Suketsune, and the two brothers who struggle to assert their rights against these forces. It is not simply a struggle between evil and good, but between the more powerful and the less powerful. It is a conflict between the forces of society--the kind of theme that was so important in classical Japanese drama in general.

What made the Soga sekai of nō and kōwaka special, however, was the way in which the character of Gorō was treated. In plays like Chōbuku Soga and Wada sakamori, we see the first steps toward the representation of Gorō as superman, a god-hero, symbolically connected with Fudō. As Gorō increased in stature and strength through repeated dramatizations, the contrast between him and Jūrō was firmly established. Unlike the aragoto Gorō, Jūrō came to be depicted as a rather feminine type, a character especially suited to a softer, wagoto style of kabuki.

The Soga tradition in ko-jōruri

Ko-, or old, jōruri, is the jōruri that preceded the partnership of Chikamatsu Monzaemon (1653-1724) and Takemoto Gidayū (1651-1714), and particularly their joint work on the play Shusse kagekiyo, performed in 1685. Just as the term hanare-kyōgen was most likely conceived after the idea of tsuzuki-kyōgen developed, the term ko-jōruri was used once the "new" jōruri of Chikamatsu and Takemoto Gidayū came into being.

29. Shimazu Hisamoto, "Kōwaka no Soga-mono," Kokugo to koku-bungaku, 10, No. 4 (1933), 465. "Without waiting for Kimpira jōruri, without waiting for Danjūrō I, aragoto had already begun."
30. The Sekai kōmoku lists about seventy characters in the Soga sekai.

Historically, the Soga plays of ko-jōruri follow those of nō and kōwaka.[31] Artistically, however, the Soga sekai did not develop further in ko-jōruri. The contribution of ko-jōruri to the Soga tradition was to bring it, using kōwaka texts, into the Tokugawa period. Although kōwaka declined artistically soon after the beginning of the Tokugawa period, it was "reborn" by being metamorphosed into the jōruri of that period.

At the same time the popular edition (rufu-bon) of the Soga monogatari was being published in the early seventeenth century, ko-jōruri Soga playbooks (shōhon) were also printed.[32] The earliest known examples of these are Ko-sode Soga, used by the reciter Satsuma Dayū (or Jōun; 1595-1672), and thought to have been printed some time before 1650, and Wada sakamori also used by Satsuma Dayū, and dated the first month of 1664. According to Takano Masami, these texts are almost exactly the same as the kōwaka texts of the same names.[33]

Another ko-jōruri Soga play is Ō-Soga Fuji kari, performed by Inoue Harima-no-Jō (1632-1685), a composite of the kōwaka Yo-uchi Soga and Jūban-giri. The reciter Uji Kaga-no-Jō (1635-1711) also performed Soga works, but until Chikamatsu began writing for him, his Soga works are almost duplicates of those of Harima-no-Jō, although Uji Kaga-no-Jō progressed beyond the Soga works of kōwaka. They simply lifted sections from the popular edition of the Soga monogatari, which, in any case, was probably closely related to the Soga plays of kōwaka.[34]

A final noteworthy feature of the Soga tradition in ko-jōruri is the existence of a cycle of seven Soga works which are among the best examples of ko-jōruri.[35] Their dates and authorship are unclear, although Watsuji

31. Even before Chikamatsu began working with Takemoto Gidayū, he had already influenced the development of jōruri by means of a work on the subject of the Soga brothers' revenge. His first known jōruri piece is Yotsugi Soga. Because this came after Danjūrō I's Soga plays had already reached the kabuki stage, it is not necessary to consider Chikamatsu's Soga plays here. This is not to deny, however, that his treatment of the Soga tradition is an important topic in jōruri studies and in drama studies in general. Evidence of its importance is the number of studies devoted to it. See, for example, the extensive treatment of the topic in Takano Masami, Kinsei engeki no kenkyū (Tokyo: Tōkyōdō, 1941).
32. Unlike kabuki, the scripts of jōruri were published for the use of the general public.
33. Takano Masami, Kinsei engeki no kenkyū, p. 36.
34. Ibid., p. 39.
35. Ko-jōruri shōhon shū, ed. Yokoyama Shigeru (Tokyo: Kadokawa Shoten, 1964), II, 490.

Tetsurō says that the author is Inoue Harima-no-Jō, which, if so, would then make him the principal "author" of Soga ko-jōruri.[36]

Ichikawa Danjūrō I and the Representation
of Soga Gorō in Kabuki

Ichikawa Danjūrō I made Soga Gorō into a god-hero for the people of Edo. To do this he used the tradition that had built up behind Gorō in other dramatic forms and combined it with acting techniques inspired by Kimpira jōruri, a form of ko-jōruri which flourished in Edo in the mid-seventeenth century. Danjūrō's achievement may be summarized in the word aragoto—for he was the founder of the "rough" style of kabuki, which not only made Edo kabuki distinctive from the wagoto, or "gentle," style of Kamigata kabuki, but also helped make kabuki as a whole a distinctive form of world drama.

Aragoto, which was largely based on and represented by Soga plays, particularly the character Soga Gorō,[37] was characterized by "the exaggerated movement and bombastic language appropriate to the superhuman prowess of warrior heroes"[38] such as Gorō. The exaggerated movement and bombastic language survive today, but audiences are less responsive to the superhuman prowess of warrior heroes, which once made fantastic action and style of speech necessary and appropriate.

36. Watsuji, Nihon geijutsu-shi kenkyū: kabuki to ayatsuri-jōruri, p. 528.
    The cycle is reprinted in Ko-jōruri shōhon shū and is based mainly on editions from the Meireki era (mid-seventeenth century), although two works are based on reprints from the Genroku era. Watsuji views this cycle as an attempt at asserting Soga jōruri in the face of the growing popularity of Kimpira jōruri in the seventeenth century. The cycle is divided into seven plays so that one play may be performed on each of seven days.
37. See Gunji, "Aragoto no seiritsu," in his Kabuki: yōshiki to denshō (Tokyo: Gakugei Shorin, 1969), p. 16, for a reference to Soga Gorō as the aragoto hero par excellence.
38. James R. Brandon, William P. Malm, and Donald H. Shively, Studies in Kabuki: Its Acting, Music, and Historical Context (Hawaii: The University Press of Hawaii, 1978), p. 40.

Interpreting the Soga Tradition: The Aragoto Hero as God-Hero

Kimpira jōruri and aragoto

Danjūrō I performed the role of Soga Gorō in the play Kachidoki homare Soga (1675) when he was sixteen years old. His stage career, however, had actually begun two years earlier, when, according the the Kabuki nendaiki, he performed the role of the legendary strongman and monster-slayer, Sakata no Kintoki, in the play Shitennō osanadachi.[39] The text of the work does not survive, but this performance marks the beginning of the aragoto style of kabuki.[40]

Shitennō osanadachi was part of the Shitennō tradition, which provided the basis and much material for Kimpira jōruri. Kimpira jōruri was brought to Edo from Kyoto by Sugiyama Shichirōzaemon (dates unknown), Satsuma Dayū, and other jōruri reciters. It was given its distinctive features by Satsuma Dayū's pupil Izumi Tayū (dates unknown), who in 1662 took the rather imposing name Sakurai Tamba no Shōjō Taira no Masanobu, and his son Izumi Tayū II.

In drama the Shitennō tradition goes back to such nō plays as Shuten Dōji and Ōeyama, which dramatize how Minamoto no Raikō, together with the shitennō,[41] Watanabe no Tsuna, Sakata no Kintoki, Usui no Sadamitsu, and Urabe no Suetake, along with the warrior Hirai Yasumasa, went to Mount Ōe where they subdued the monster Shuten Dōji. Until the Tokugawa period the popularity of the Shitennō tradition came close to that of the Soga and Gikeiki traditions.[42]

Kimpira jōruri made extensive use of the exploits of Sakata no Kintoki's son, Kimpira, who like his father was brave and strong. Kimpira jōruri was a violent type of dramatic presentation, both in the rough style of jōruri delivery and in the way puppets were made to enact great battle scenes culminating in houses being tossed up in the air, trees being torn out by the roots, and enemies having their heads and various limbs ripped from their bodies. Danjūrō, who was a youth when Kimpira jōruri was at the height of its

---

39. Tachikawa, (Hana no Edo) Kabuki nendaiki, p. 15.
40. Ibid. See Suwa Haruo, Genroku kabuki no kenkyū (Tokyo: Kasama Shoin, 1967), p. 363, for an entry slightly different from that in the Nendaiki.
41. The word shitennō (the four tennō) originally referred to the Buddhist deities who guarded each of the four directions. In Japanese culture the word came to be applied generally to any group of four outstanding personages. Minamoto no Raikō's four tennō are perhaps the most famous shitennō.
42. See Kawatake, Nihon engeki zenshi, p. 440.

popularity, was reportedly influenced by it and later adapted some of its techniques to kabuki.

When Danjūrō appeared on stage for the first time as Kintoki, his style of acting and make-up were at least in part derived from Kimpira jōruri.[43] He did a fight scene (tachi-mawari) wielding an ax in one hand, and painted his whole body red with crimson and black lines decorating his face[44]—thereby beginning the style of make-up that came to be known as kumadori, which is now one of the distinguishing features of aragoto.

From the outset these and other such techniques appealed greatly to Edo audiences. Their effect was powerful and shocking, exactly what the residents of the samurai city wanted. Danjūrō, however, needed something more than what Kimpira jōruri provided in order to establish the style that would determine the course of kabuki. What he needed was found in the Soga tradition, which had by the early Tokugawa period given much material to other dramatic forms.

Soga Gorō as God-Hero

Soga Gorō was the aragoto hero par excellence. But the display of physical strength and the bold presentation coming from Kimpira jōruri were not the most important elements in the power he had when represented on stage by Danjūrō. His power came from the belief audiences had that he was a god-hero. To understand this, we must look at the role of the hito-gami, "man-god," in kabuki.

Yanagita Kunio first suggested the importance of a connection between hito-gami and kabuki when he said that the name Gorō, which is used for several aragoto kabuki heroes (such as Soga Gorō and Kamakura Gongorō), actually stands for goryō.[45] As defined by Hori Ichirō,

> Originally, the goryō were the malevolent spirits of noble persons who died in political intrigues. They were associated with disasters, epidemics, and wars. . . . Originally, the belief in goryō

---

43. In "Aragoto no seiritsu," p. 15, Gunji says that Danjūrō I got a "hint" for aragoto from Kimpira jōruri.
44. Tachikawa, (Hana no Edo) Kabuki nendaiki, p. 15.
45. According to Gunji, "Aragoto no seiritsu," p. 18, this was first suggested by Yanagita in his essay "Imōto no chikara."

> was also influenced by the Chinese idea that if the spirits of the dead did not have memorial services performed by their descendants, they would become evil spirits or demons. . . . The belief in goryō was also influenced by the Buddhist idea that every human being has Buddha nature within him and thus has the possibility of becoming a Buddha. Later, the idea of goryō was gradually expanded through the reinterpretation that even an ordinary person could become a goryō or goryō-shin (goryō deity) by his own will power, ardent wish on the verge of death, or accidental death under unusual circumstances.

> Belief in goryō . . . has . . . survived in folk beliefs, rituals, and customs as well as in folk arts, dancing, and music. Even the most refined classical dramas or plays are thought to have originated from the belief in goryō or the hito-gami complex.[46]

The belief that a person has the potential to become a god or acquire god-like power is what underlies the concepts of goryō and hito-gami.[47] Knowledge of these beliefs, which were still important and influential during the Tokugawa period, has helped develop a new view of aragoto and its heroes.[48]

The most famous hito-gami or goryō in history was Sugawara no Michizane (845-903), a nobleman who died in exile after being accused of plotting against the emperor. Some twenty years after he died—a period in which many disasters struck Kyoto that were attributed to Sugawara's vengeful spirit—Sugawara was enshrined at Kitano Shrine in Kyoto and worshipped as a god throughout the country. It was presumed that such worship would appease the angry spirit. Sugawara was a nobleman, but samurai and commoners could also become superhuman beings.[49] Soga Gorō is perhaps the most famous example of such a being without noble lineage.

46. Hori Ichirō, in Joseph M. Kitagawa and Alan L. Miller (eds.), Folk Religion in Japan: Continuity and Change (Chicago: University of Chicago Press, 1968), pp. 43-44.
47. For our purposes here, goryō and hito-gami stand for essentially the same concept.
48. Particularly Gunji. Mention should also be made here of an article by Umehara Takeshi called "The Genealogy of Avenging Spirits," translated by Susanna Contini, Diogenes, No. 84 (1974), 17-30, the thesis of which is that the concept of avenging spirits forms the basis of Japanese civilization. It is a general summary of the ideas of Origuchi Shinobu and his disciples.
49. The belief that a man could somehow become a god is a universal phenomenon:
> Even in the conscious period there was the tradition that gods were men of a previous age who had died. Hesiod speaks of a

The belief in goryō required that the spirit be appeased through worship. It is very interesting, however, that worship of the spirits of the departed did not just take the form of enshrinement, but could also take the form of dramatic performances based on the lives of the god-heroes. Dramatic performances include the telling of oral tales in the Muromachi period, which were largely concerned with the story of the Soga brothers. Ruch has said that "Muromachi vocal literature was more than entertainment or diversion; it was a magico-religious and psychotherapeutic ceremony for artist and audience."[50] It may be similarly said of kabuki in the Tokugawa period. In the world of pre-modern Japan both telling stories and performing dramas about heroes were ways to entertain audiences and ways to worship those heroes and acknowledge their powers. Danjūrō I brought together these aspects on the kabuki stage.

This special way of viewing dramatic character also helps in understanding the nature of the principle of tradition in kabuki, and the continuity in Japanese culture that underlies it. In short, Soga Gorō's story had to be told and at the same time because it was told it began to acquire a kind of momentum that would carry it through various transformations--from oral narrative, to nō and kōwaka, and on to ko-jōruri (and jōruri), and kabuki forms. Soga Gorō acquired importance and, by extension, god-likeness for the very reason that his story was repeatedly told. It became so central to the culture that it formed part of what Ruch has called the national literature.

As mentioned, the first entry in the Kabuki nempyō refers to Okuni performing Soga plays. Okuni began kabuki by doing nembutsu (a prayer to Amida Buddha) songs and dances. Hori says:

> the practice of Nenbutsu . . . and the belief in Amida-butsu to whom Nenbutsu was offered as a prayer appeared in about the ninth century and flourished in the tenth and eleventh centuries;

> golden race of men who preceded his own generation and became the "holy demons upon the earth, beneficent, averters of ills, guardians of mortal men." Similar references can be found up to four centuries later, as when Plato refers to heroes who after death become the demons that tell people what to do.
> Julian Jaynes, The Origin of Consciousness in the Breakdown of the Bicameral Mind (Boston: Houghton Mifflin, 1977), p. 164.

50. Ruch, "Medieval Jongleurs and the Making of a National Literature," p. 306.

they were connected with the rising belief in goryō. Many
magical Nenbutsu dances and dramas still exist in rural villages.
They have the function of driving off evil spirits of the dead . . .
(in time) popular Nenbutsu beliefs and practices degenerated into
magico-artistic   entertainments   and   lost   their   religious
character.[51]

Even though the religious character may have been lost--just as the
agricultural connection was lost in the case of the dramatic calendar—some
entertainments did start as "magic against the goryō."[52] It can be supposed
that kabuki at least in part had this magical function when Okuni performed.

Thus, why Okuni may have performed Soga plays can be understood
even if the fact cannot actually be proven. She would have done them as part
of a _nembutsu_ ritual, albeit secularized and carried out mainly for
entertainment purposes. And that is how drama has generally started—with
the carrying out of some religious ritual which in time moved out of the realm
of religion and into the realm of "pure" drama.

Just as goryō is linked with Gorō (according to Yanagita), the word ara-
hito-gami may be linked with aragoto. Although the ara in both words is
usually interpreted as "violent," "angry," or simply "rough," there is another
way to read its meaning and that is in the sense of "existence" or "appearance."[53] Despite the seeming disparity of these interpretations, I think it
is very important that both be considered together. The latter tells us that a
being, namely the god-hero, exists and that he can appear before us in human
form. The implication of this for the drama is that this being may be
represented by a human actor on a stage. The former then gives us an idea of
the being's nature, which is that he is strong and prone to violent displays of
strength.

Thus, we have in the aragoto hero a representation of a superhuman
being—or god-hero—in human form. In his portrayals of Soga Gorō, Kimpira,
Kintoki, Kamakura Gongorō, and others, Danjūrō I brought this kind of being
to the kabuki stage. The kumadori make-up and the mie poses were Danjūrō's
way of giving himself a fierce and awe-inspiring presence like that of Fudō or
like the statues that guard Buddhist temples, whose aggressive stances and
violent expressions are often compared to those of the aragoto hero.

51. Hori, Folk Religion in Japan: Continuity and Change, p. 73.
52. Ibid., p. 74.
53. This alternative reading was suggested to me in a conversation with
Gunji. The analysis that follows, however, is mine.

Danjūrō's characters may have been fictional, but his portrayals of them were real and from the beginning audiences responded enthusiastically to them. Having first seen the technical possibility of bringing "ara" characters to the stage in Kimpira jōruri, Danjūrō then brought them to the kabuki stage. He did this by means of the Soga sekai and the popular beliefs that lay behind it, thus creating the god-hero Gorō who could be continually transformed and renewed by later generations of Danjūrōs.[54]

The Soga Tradition and the Kabuki Calendar

Records show that Danjūrō's first Soga play, Kachidoki homare Soga, was produced beginning in the fifth month of 1675.[55] In fact, with one exception,[56] plays which featured Danjūrō as Soga Gorō began in the fifth month of the year.[57] Although the traditional starting date for the bon production period came to be in the middle of the seventh month, in the Genroku era--when Danjūrō I was active--productions beginning in the fifth month were thought of as bon productions. This is shown by an entry in the Yakusha mannenreki, a critique published in 1700, which says that every year Soga plays were performed during the bon (i.e., beginning in the fifth month) production period.[58] From about 1703 (a year before Danjūrō I was killed on stage by a fellow actor), Soga plays began to be used for spring productions, and in 1709 all theaters in Edo featured Soga plays as spring productions.[59] From that time on, spring productions in Edo were based on the Soga tradition.

Why Soga plays were first used for bon productions and then used for spring productions is not entirely clear. There is no dobut, however, that either season was appropriate. As the entry in the Yakusha mannenreki also says, the purpose of Soga plays was to worship the souls of the dead brothers.[60] In Japan the two special seasons of the year for honoring

---

54. Speaking of renewal, it may also be noted that a third possible interpretation of ara is "new."
55. Ihara, Kabuki nempyō, I, p. 123.
56. The exception was Kokon kyōdai tsuwamono Soga, which was produced in the third month.
57. Two examples are Tsuwamono kongen Soga, produced in 1697, and Dainihon tekkai sennin, produced in 1700.
58. Yakusha mannenreki, in Kabuki hyōbanki shūsei, ed. Kabuki Hyōbanki Kenkyūkai (Tokyo: Iwanami Shoten, 1974), II, 518.
59. See Chapter I, note 27.
60. Yakusha mannenreki, 518.

departed spirits are New Year's (i.e., spring) and bon. Portraying the Soga brothers in drama was one way of honoring them. Moreover, since the brothers carried out their revenge between the seasons of spring and bon, it was logical to have plays which concerned the revenge either begin or end at those times. Whether produced at the time of bon, as they were at first, or whether produced during the spring, as they came to be, Soga plays were a fixed part of the traditional calendar.

An Example of Danjūrō I's Representation
of Soga Gorō: Tsuwamono kongen Soga

   Tsuwamono kongen Soga is a good example of Danjūrō I's representation of Soga Gorō. One of the major plays in which Danjūrō portrayed Soga Gorō, it survives as an e-iri kyōgen-bon, an illustrated playbook of the Genroku era.[61] Among the illustrations are several excellent ones which show Danjūrō as the archetypal aragoto Soga Gorō. Moreover, an incident associated with it reveals the god-hero nature of Danjūrō's Soga Gorō. Finally, it is the play in which Danjūrō II, who will be discussed in the next chapter, made his stage debut.

   Danjūrō as Gorō was a true aragoto figure. He has the upper part of his kimono pulled down and the lower part tucked up. This allowed him freedom of movement, but more importantly, it conveyed the sense of Gorō's physical strength by letting the audience get a good view of the actor's body. He is shown with protruding eyes, a turned-down, tooth-baring mouth, and with one leg aggressively thrust forward.

   The kind of transformation that Danjūrō carried out in the Soga tradition is best seen in that part of Tsuwamono kongen Soga which tells the same story as the nō Chōbuku Soga. After Gorō has met his enemy Kudō Suketsune for the first time, his only thought is to carry out the revenge as soon as possible. But the time is not right and he must wait. In the nō play the priest takes over at this point and prays to Fudō on behalf of Gorō. This

61. Tsuwamono kongen Soga is included in Genroku kabuki kessaku shū, pp. 55-91.
   Playbooks are not complete texts. Instead, they are recapitulations of plays using a narrative format, though containing many lines of what seems to be actual dialogue. Illustrations, of course, are important parts of these works. For twenty pages of text in Tsuwamono kongen Soga, there are twelve pages of illustrations showing scenes from the play. More than words, these pictures communicate the spirit of actual performance.

results in the appearance of Fudō who assures everyone that in time Gorō will be granted the strength to carry out the deed. In Tsuwamono kongen Soga, however, Fudō's intentions are more graphically shown. Gorō undergoes thirty-seven days of religious austerities (aragyō, literally "rough action"; note the ara which is the same as that in aragoto and ara-hito-gami). He acquires fantastic strength and as proof of this he pulls out a large bamboo by its roots. (This famous scene is called Takenuki Soga, the bamboo-pulling Soga.) As in the case of Chōbuku Soga, Fudō also makes his appearance here. Danjūrō's son, Kuzō, who later became Danjūrō II, played the role of Fudō.[62] The close tie between Gorō and Fudō was thus heightened by the underlying family relationship of Danjūrō and his son. Undoubtedly, this intensified the effect of the play.[63] When Tsuwamono kongen Soga was being performed, people flocked to the theater from Narita (in present-day Chiba Prefecture) with money they had collected to present to Danjūrō.[64] It was as if they viewed Danjūrō and his son themselves as god-heroes—as actual manifestations of Gorō and Fudō. Following this zealous display, the actors led a procession out to Shinshōji temple in Narita (where Fudō is worshipped) and in turn contributed money there.[65] It is said that from that time the Danjūrō line of actors began to be referred to as "Narita-ya" (House of Narita).[66] Later on Fudō lost his immediate association with Gorō, but in the beginning that association helped build up the power of the character Gorō.

62. Kuzō first appeared in the play in the role of the mountain priest (yamabushi) Tsūrikibō, who at the end of the third part of the play, is transformed into Fudō. Ibid., p. 56.
63. An interesting aspect of the e-iri kyōgen-bon illustration of Gorō and Fudō is its resemblance to honji-suijaku-type Shintō paintings, which depict a Buddhist deity and his Shintō counterpart. If we look at the illustration in this way, Fudō and Gorō can be interpreted as one and the same. This further strengthens the argument that has been put forward thus far. For discussions of the theory of honji-suijaku and its application to Shintō painting, see Alicia Matsunaga, The Buddhist Philosophy of Assimilation: The Historical Development of the Honji-Suijaku Theory (Rutland, Vermont: Charles E. Tuttle, 1969), and Kageyama Haruki, The Arts of Shinto, translated and adapted by Christine Guth (New York: Weatherhill, 1973).
64. Nishiyama, Ichikawa Danjūrō, p. 18.
65. Ibid.
66. Ibid.

Chapter 4

SUKEROKU, FLOWER OF EDO:
THE TRANSFORMATION OF SOGA GORO INTO SUKEROKU

Sukeroku is set at the Miura-ya,[1] in the Yoshiwara gay quarters in Edo. There Sukeroku confronts Ikyū when both arrive expecting to meet Agemaki, a grand courtesan of the quarters. Although Ikyū is a powerful, albeit blustery, samurai with a retinue of underlings to do his bidding, Agemaki is enamoured of the townsman Sukeroku. In one of the most famous speeches of the play, she says of the two men: "Compare Sukeroku and Ikyū, side by side. Here is the one, a young stag, here is the other, an old crab. White and black, like snow and ink. One the broad ocean, one a mire of mud; one deep, one shallow, as the courtesan's beloved and the prostitute's customer."[2]

The confrontation between Sukeroku and Ikyū could be seen simply as the rivalry of two men from different classes of society over the affections of the same woman, if it were not for the revelation that Sukeroku is really the samurai Soga Gorō. The play, in fact, is not about class rivalry as much as it is about matters of identity and revenge. Gorō has come into the gay quarters in the identity of Sukeroku to search for the stolen sword that he must have to carry out the revenge. The sword he is looking for is Tomokirimaru, which was a gift from Yoshitsune. Gorō's aim is to provoke samurai passing through the quarters to draw their weapons so that he can check to see whether they have the one he is looking for. As Sukeroku he can do this without raising suspicion about the revenge. Ikyū, who has the sword, is actually the Heike general Iga Heinai Zaemon.

---

1. The Miura-ya was an ageya (Kabuki jūachi-ban shū, ed. Gunji, p. 78), a place where courtesans entertained their guests. Courtesans did not live in ageya.
2. "Sukeroku: Flower of Edo," in Kabuki: Five Classic Plays, translated by James R. Brandon (Cambridge: Harvard University Press, 1975), p. 61.

Once Agemaki, her friend Shiratama, and the other courtesans of the Miura-ya, and Ikyū and his men have been introduced, Sukeroku enters by performing his famous dance on the hanamichi.   The chorus sings in accompaniment:

Hear the shamisen sounding bright Sugagaki;
Arousing our memories in the gay quarter . . .
Impregnated kimono crest of Five Seasons;
Symbol of year's waiting, steeped deeply in love . . .
Do not hurry, do not rush;
The world is transient, a wheel that turns;
Time passes day by day as expected . . .[3]
You are charming! You are marvellous![3]

Sukeroku's coming had been eagerly awaited by all the courtesans.   Each welcomes him by offering him a pipe to smoke.   In contrast, Ikyū, who is sitting nearby, receives nothing.   And when he protests, Sukeroku insults him by "handing" him a pipe stuck between his toes.

The pipe scene is followed by a scene involving a noodle vendor, Sukeroku, Kampera Mombei (a samurai retainer of Ikyū), and Mombei's servant Asagao Sembei.   When Mombei comes out of the Miura-ya drunk and out of sorts because no courtesan came to serve him in the bath, a noodle vendor accidentally bumps into him. Mombei reacts by preparing to strike him. It is a classic case of samurai versus commoner. Sukeroku, however, steps in on behalf of the vendor and tells Mombei to forgive him. Since Sukeroku to all appearances is not a samurai, he has no right to tell Mombei what to do. An argument then breaks out between them and ends when Sukeroku dumps a bowl of noodles on Mombei's head. Mombei is shown for a fool when, thinking that the noodles are actually his brains, he cries out that he has been mortally wounded.   Once the situation is made clear he orders his gang to attack Sukeroku. Sukeroku, however, turns out to be so imposing that they slink away without touching him. Even when Sembei tries to attack Sukeroku, he is easily driven back.

Neither Sembei nor Mombei can understand who Sukeroku is.   In contrast to the samurai style Mombei uses to identify himself in the heat of his confrontation with Sukeroku ("Taking the Kan of my name from from Kan'u, the Chinese general of the Three Kingdoms whose flowing Cloud Beard reminds us of Lord Ikyū, and the Mon of my name signifying a treasured temple gate, I am the samurai Kampera Mombei, wealthy powerful Kampera

3. Ibid., pp. 62-63.

Mombei!"[4]), Sukeroku takes his time before he finally tells everyone in his characteristic akutai ("insult") style:

> No one but an ass sets foot in Yoshiwara not knowing my name. So hear it well. A headband of purple, the pride of Edo, dyed in Edo, binds my hair, the strands of which as you look through them frame a face which, if it graced a ukiyoe print, would make that picture famous in Japan! Who does not know this dragon in the water growing stronger as his enemies increase? From the carousers at the pleasure houses of the Golden Dragon Mountain to the grim image of the ferocious god Fudō in Meguro, all Edo's eight-hundred-and-eight districts do not hide the man who does not know this wearer of the blossoms of Yoshiwara, this youthful Sukeroku, Agemaki's Sukeroku! Scum! Bow before this face! Worship it![5]

Sukeroku is the quintessential man of Edo. Words are his best weapon. He has manipulated Sembei and Mombei by his actions and extravagant introduction of himself. Frightened, they do exactly as Sukeroku wants them to do. They draw their swords, which he has a chance to inspect before chasing them away.

Sukeroku's identity as Soga Gorō is clearly revealed to the audience in a scene with his brother, Jūrō, who also has another identity—that of the sake peddler, Shimbei. In the effeminate and un-samurai-like Shimbei, we see a parody of the wagoto Jūrō. Shimbei upbraids Sukeroku:

> Every day mother and I heard stories of your fighting in Yoshiwara . . . . The day the crows don't caw is the day Sukeroku doesn't fight in Yoshiwara, they say. She could not believe this wastrel called Sukeroku was her son, Gorō. So she sent me to the quarter to see . . . . For eighteen years we have waited to avenge father's murder at Hakone Mountain, but now that the time has come, you disgrace yourself with quarreling and debauchery. Honor your parents is the first precept of morality, honor your elder brother is the second. You esteem neither. The bond between us is broken. You are no longer my brother Gorō.[6]

4. Ibid., p. 69.
5. Ibid., pp. 71–72.
6. Ibid., p. 75.

But Sukeroku replies that he only fights out of his filial duty, for the purpose of finding the stolen sword. Shimbei (Jūrō) is convinced and decides to join his brother in his search.

The play continues with two comic scenes in which the brothers encounter first two country samurai and then a gay quarters dandy. Both the samurai bumpkins and the dandy let Sukeroku get the best of them—the former because they are ignorant in the ways of the city and the latter because he is overly clever and effete.

A more serious chord is then struck when the brothers are discovered by their mother, who has come into the Yoshiwara disguised as a samurai. Thinking that both of her sons are now engaged in questionable behavior in the gay quarters, she admonishes them: "Virtuous sons would be taking vengeance on their father's slayer. My sons take aliases and brawl in public places."[7] The mother is finally appeased when she hears their explanation.

The play ends with the last encounter between Sukeroku and Ikyū. Ikyū, who has discovered that Sukeroku is Soga Gorō, draws his sword in a moment of emotion, and Sukeroku sees that he has Tomokirimaru. Ikyū swears that he will never part with the sword. (As a Heike general he plans to use the sword that once belonged to Minamoto no Yoshitsune to destroy the Minamoto clan.) He attacks Sukeroku, who kills him and takes possession of the sword. The play closes with Sukeroku and Agemaki waiting for nightfall in order to escape from the Yoshiwara and to go on to find the brothers' enemy, Suketsune.

The Origins of the Sukeroku Innovation

When Sukeroku was performed for the first time by Ichikawa Danjūrō II in 1713, the play was new to the Edo kabuki stage, thus fulfilling a primary requirement of an innovation. However, the play was not completely new. Previously, the story of Sukeroku and Agemaki had been an extablished theme of Kamigata kabuki and, especially, jōruri. In creating his own Sukeroku,[8] Danjūrō removed the love suicide element, and put the focus instead on Sukeroku as a pure Edo character.

7. Ibid., p. 81.
8. Danjūrō II doubtlessly worked with one or more playwrights, but their identity is the subject of much controversy. Many suggest Tsuuchi Jihei II (1679-1760).

The importance of the Kamigata origins of Sukeroku is threefold. First, they reaffirm a point about the creative processes of Japanese dramatic arts that was made earlier: that what is "new" in one art form may be based on themes and characters that are already known in another art form. Second, they are reminders that in the early eighteenth century the Kamigata area was still the center of Japanese culture, but just as Sukeroku shifted to Edo, so was the center of culture moving there as well. And third, they show the divergent interests of Kamigata and Edo audiences: whereas the former wanted their Sukeroku to be a tragic lover, the latter wanted theirs to be a triumphant hero.

The story of Sukeroku and Agemaki was dramatized in the Kamigata area as early as 1678, thirty-five years before the first production of Sukeroku in Edo by Danjūrō II, in the play Yorozuya Sukeroku shinjū.[9] This was followed by a number of other works, including Kyō Sukeroku shinjū (1707), Semi no nukegara (1707), and Sennichi-dera shinjū (1709).[10]

How Danjūrō II became acquainted with the Kamigata Sukeroku is still being debated. It is commonly believed, however, that the jōruri reciter Miyako Itchū journeyed from the Kamigata area to Edo in 1712 and performed one or more of the works mentioned above, which Danjūrō II heard and then had made into a work for himself.[11]

Mention should also be made of a theory that there was actually someone named Sukeroku living in Edo, who was the model for Danjūrō.[12] Stories about a real Sukeroku, however, sound more like versions of later kabuki plays than actual historical accounts.

Ichikawa Danjūrō II and the Introduction of the Sukeroku Innovation to Edo Kabuki

In his lifetime Danjūrō II performed the role of Sukeroku three times. The first was in 1713, as part of the play Hana-yakata Aigo-zakura. The

9. Atsumi, "Sukeroku no yurai," Engei gahō, March 1925, pp. 26-54; reprinted in (Kokuritsu Gekijō) Jōen shiryō shū, No. 134 (January 1977), p. 35.
10. Ibid.
11. Ibid., p. 36.
12. See Tachikawa, (Hana no Edo) Kabuki nendaiki, p. 38, which says that there was a grave of someone by the name of Hanakawado no Sukeroku (which is the same as Sukeroku's full name in the play) in the Shintorigoe igyō-in (temple) in Edo.

second was in 1716 in Shikirei yawaragi Soga. And the third was in 1749, as part of Otoko-moji Soga monogatari.[13] For his first Sukeroku Danjūrō was twenty-five; for his last—his so-called ichidai issei performance—he was sixty-one.

In studying the three productions which constitute Danjūrō II's introduction of the Sukeroku innovation to Edo kabuki, one is also following the development of Danjūrō II's career, as he grew from a young man who had just begun to show his potential to a fully mature man at the top of his profession. What makes these three productions even more significant is that they also parallel the development of what came to be thought of as the characteristic culture of Edo—that is, the culture of the so-called Edokko, or "child of Edo." The word Edokko was an expression of pride. It was not only pride in growing up and living in the city of Edo (for regardless of place of birth only the townsman-commoner, the chōnin, could be an Edokko), but also pride in a certain manner and style of living. Such pride was represented by Danjūrō II in his portrayals of Sukeroku.[14]

Danjūrō II's first Sukeroku: Before the Soga Connection

Danjūrō II first performed Sukeroku in the third month of 1713 at the Yamamura-za. He wore a kimono of black pongee and a headband of reddish-yellow cotton. The action focused on a great roof-top fight scene between Sukeroku and Ikyū and his men, with Ikyū being killed in the end.[15]

The clearest image of this first Sukeroku comes from an illustration found in Sukeroku kyōgenko by Santō Kyōden (1761-1816).[16] Kyōden attributes the picture to the artist Kondō Sukegorō Kiyoharu (fl. early

13. The three play titles given here are ō-nadai. In 1749 the Sukeroku section was performed under the title Sukeroku kuruwa no ie-zakara, which is actually the title of the jōruri piece used as the accompaniment for Sukeroku's dance entrance.
    There is some dispute about the ō-nadai title of the play that was produced in 1713. Kawatake, Nihon engeki zenshi, p. 513, calls it Hana-yakata Aigo no waka.
14. The term Edokko is vague and wide-ranging, and it appears that the best way to appreciate the flavor of it is to study Sukeroku. As the Meiji writer Sasagawa Rimpū said, "Those who do not understand Sukeroku do not understand the spirit of Edo." Quoted in Nishiyama, Edo chōnin no kenkyū (Tokyo: Yoshikawa Kōbunkan, 1973), II, 14.
15. Atsumi, "Sukeroku no yurai," p. 37.
16. Santō Kyōden, Sukeroku kyōgen-kō, in Kinsei kiseki-kō (1804; reprinted in Nihon zuihitsu zenshū, Tokyo: Kokumin Tosho, 1929, Vol. 11, 125-28.

eighteenth century), and it only survives in Kyōden's work. Sukeroku has his kimono top pulled down, leaving the upper part of his body bare. His muscles are bulging and his legs are thrust out. The pose is that of the aragoto hero. This Sukeroku seems out of place in the gay quarters; we can see the striking similarity between him and Soga Gorō in Tsuwamono kongen Soga.

Sukeroku, however, was not a totally aragoto figure. An entry in the Yakusha irokeizu, a critique published in the second month of 1714, says that he was an aragoto satte nuregoto gakari otokodate.[17] This means that the aragoto style, which normally characterized representations of otokodate, was dispensed with and Sukeroku was instead an otokodate in the nuregoto style. Nuregoto, which is related to, but not the same as, the wagoto, or "gentle" style, of kabuki, is an erotic type of presentation--associated with lovers, not heroes. In time Sukeroku came to be represented as a physically attractive character as well as an awe-inspiring one. This was the result of refinements made by Danjūrō II in his father's aragoto art. It is important to realize, however, that from the beginning the style of production (if we use the illustration as evidence) was very much in the heroic tradition and despite outward changes that style always remained a significant part of the play. Surely it is not a coincidence that Soga Gorō, the first Sukeroku, and Danjūrō's later Sukerokus are all shown in exactly the same way--with one leg thrust forward, attacking the enemy or appearing ready to attack, and with a determined expression on the face. The god-hero nature is consistently present in all of these depictions.

The similarity between Soga Gorō and the first Sukeroku has been suggested, but Sukeroku was not yet part of the Soga tradition. As the title Hana-yakata Aigo-zakura indicates, the play was based on the Aigo tradition. Although we know the Aigo tradition treated of themes of feudal family rivalry, there is unfortunately no extant play which uses Aigo material.

Why was Sukeroku first made part of a play not in the Soga tradition-- especially since records show that the play was performed in the third month of the year and should therefore be expected to be part of the theater's spring production, which was usually in the Soga world.

There are two ways to answer this. First, as was pointed out above, the Yamamura-za did not have a proper spring production in 1713. Its kao-mise production had started in the first month of the new year--two months

---

17. Yakusha irokeizu, in Kabuki hyōbanki shūsei, ed. Kabuki Hyōbanki Kenkyūkai (Tokyo: Iwanami Shoten, 1974), Vol. 5, 409.

late—and it was not until the third month (or possibly later, according to some accounts) that the spring production actually began. Second, kabuki structure at that time was just emerging from its formative period and although theater managers were generally inclined to produce Soga plays in the spring, exceptions could be made. Also, plays based on the Aigo tradition seem to have been popular just at that time; in the following year, 1714, Danjūrō again did an Aigo play at the Morita-za.[18]

Despite the lack of a Soga connection in 1713, Sukeroku had a double identity. Sukeroku's other identity was the samurai Daidōji Tahatanosuke, and Shirazake-uri Shimbei (who was later Jūrō) was a samurai named Araki Saemon.

Aside from Sukeroku and Shimbei, who were to continue as major characters in later Sukeroku plays, the other characters who appeared in this first Sukeroku were: Agemaki, Ikyū, Sukeroku's mother (sometimes known as Mankō), Sembei, Keisei Kisegawa (the courtesan Kisegawa, who later became Shiratama), and Kantera Mombei (later, Kampera Mombei).

The importance of this first Sukeroku is that it brought the Sukeroku innovation to the Edo kabuki stage and established the setting and general character constellation for all later Sukeroku plays. Moreover, in terms of dramatic structure, it was one of the pioneering plays in which the major sections of a long play were linked together, as is evidenced by Sukeroku's double identity as otokodate and samurai.

In costume, acting style, and, no doubt, contents, the first Sukeroku was very different from the way it is now. What is important about it, however, is that it passed the crucial test of its first production. If it did not have potential as a good play, it would never have been heard of again. Instead, it was taken out of the Aigo world and survived as part of a Soga play.

Danjūrō II's second Sukeroku: the Soga Connection

Danjūrō II performed Sukeroku for the second time in the second month of 1716 at the Nakamura-za. This was the turning point in the production of the play; many elements of the staging and costumes that are still associated with Sukeroku, including the connection with the Soga tradition, were established at this time.[19] This second Sukeroku also helped preserve an

18. Ihara, Kabuki nempyō, Vol. I, p. 435.

event which happened in Edo: cherry trees were planted in the Yoshiwara gay quarters. They were immediately made part of the setting of the play, and not only fixed the seasonal association of Sukeroku but they also underscored the intimate connection between kabuki and the gay quarters.[20]

In this second Sukeroku Danjūrō used the snake's eye umbrella that is now one of Sukeroku's trademarks.[21] He also had a shakuhachi (bamboo flute) tucked into the back of his obi, which is also still used. Other changes that became standard for Sukeroku are the purple headband, which replaced the reddish-yellow one of the first production, and the black, short-sleeved kimono, which replaced the one made of black pongee.[22] Attired in a more lavish costume, Sukeroku was becoming elegant.

The most symbolic change in costume for the second production was the reported replacement of the long samurai sword with a short one, the only sword a commoner could carry.[23] There is a logical explanation for this change. When Sukeroku became Soga Gorō, as he did in this production, his reason for coming into the gay quarters and fighting with others there was that he was searching for the sword that he needed to carry out the revenge. The sword he was looking for was, of course, a long samurai sword, and it was natural then that he be carrying only a short one.

There is, however, another possible reason for his having only a short sword—that was part of the process of softening Sukeroku, of making him less like the warrior he appeared to be in the first production. Such an observation requires some mention of the difference in the aragoto art (particularly with respect to the representation of Soga Gorō) of Danjūrō I and Danjūrō II.

Danjūrō II had made his stage debut in the play Tsuwamono kongen Soga. In that work, as we have seen, Danjūrō I played a strongly aragoto Soga Gorō. Gorō was also a role that Danjūrō II made famous; in fact, it was the principle role of his acting career. Danjūrō II did almost forty Soga plays in his lifetime and many had extraordinarily long runs.[24]

19. Kawatake, Nihon engeki zenshi, p. 514.
20. For more on the connection between kabuki and the gay quarters, see Gunji, Kabuki to Yoshiwara.
21. Ihara, Kabuki nempyō, Vol. 1, p. 463.
22. Atsumi, "Sukeroku no yurai," pp. 38–39.
23. Ibid.
24. In Ichikawa Danjūrō, pp. 54–56, Nishiyama provides a chart of Danjūrō II's Soga plays.

The Gorō that Danjūrō II made famous was not, however, the same Gorō that his father had done. Danjūrō II began with his father's aragoto style and reworked it with elements of the wagoto style that Sakata Tōjūrō had developed so sucessfully in the Kamigata area. Beginning in 1711 (two years before the first Sukeroku) in the play Yunzei yome-iri Soga, instead of the red-faced Gorō of Danjūrō I, he used white make-up with red lines around the eyes.[25] This signified a new approach to the role. Whereas Soga Gorō had been totally fierce and awe-inspiring, with Danjūrō II he began to acquire a softer, more sensuous nature. From this beginning, Danjūrō II took the idea to its fullest extent five years later in the yawaragi Soga, or "gentle" Soga, of the play Shikirei yawaragi Soga (1716), which contained the second Sukeroku. Although we are again frustrated in our attempt to know the full details of the play because of the lack of a text, contemporary observers indicate that this play was a complete departure from Danjūrō I's Soga plays (even the tile, with the use of the word "gentle," indicates as much).[26] A great deal of the importance of this play, of course, can be accounted for by the fact that it was the first time that the Sukeroku innovation was joined to a Soga play.

In 1716 the main portion of Sukeroku opened, as it does now, with Sukeroku's dance-entrance on the hanamichi. In that year, it was done to the accompaniment of Edo Handayū Bushi, although other forms of jōruri, especially Katō Bushi, were later used. The characters that were introduced in the 1713 production were also in the 1716 production, though instead of being identified as a sake seller, Shimbei became an oil seller (Abura-uri Shimbei). More important, though, is that Shimbei became identified as Soga Jūrō, brother of Sukeroku/Gorō. Moreover, Agemaki here was said to be Tora no Shōshō (Gorō's lover in the Soga story).[27]

The significance of Danjūrō II's second Sukeroku is the use of the Sukeroku innovation in a Soga play and the softer approach to both Sukeroku and Soga characterization in general. Both of these aspects were continued in Danjūrō II's third and last Sukeroku.

Danjūrō II's Third Sukeroku

Whereas the first and second times that Danjūrō II did Sukeroku were the first and second times it had ever been done, by the third time, three

25. Atsumi, "Sukeroku no yurai," pp. 38-39.
26. Ihara, Kabuki nempyō, Vol. 1, pp. 463-64.
27. Ibid.

other actors had taken the leading role. All of the actors performed at the Ichimura-za, where Danjūrō had not done Sukeroku. The first was Ichimura Takenojō (dates unclear), who appeared as Sukeroku in the third month of 1733 in the play Hanafusa bunshin Soga,[28] the second was Ichikawa Danjūrō III who performed Sukeroku in the third month of 1739 in the play Hatsumotoyui kayoi Soga,[29] and the third was Onoe Kikugorō I (1717-83), who portrayed Sukeroku in the third month of 1746 in the play Kikeba mukashi Soga monogatari.[30] With each production, the play grew and developed, paving the way for the Sukeroku innovation to become the Sukeroku tradition.

The title of the work in which Danjūrō II performed his third and final Sukeroku was Otoko-moji Soga monogatari, performed in the third month of 1749 at the Nakamura-za. It is fairly certain that the playwright in this case was Fujimoto Tobun, and indeed, Kawatake Shigetoshi calls the play one of Tobun's representative works.[31]

Judging by the illustration of Sukeroku that survives from this production, and by what was been written about it, Danjūrō II's third Sukeroku was ima no Sukeroku—an "up-to-date" Sukeroku, one who had changed with the times.[32] One catalyst of change was the close association in the mid-eighteenth century between Danjūrō II (who was at the height of his career) and the wealthy Edo rice brokers (who were flourishing at that time). Not only is Sukeroku said to be modeled on Ōguchiya Gyou, a rice broker, but a change in the third production was the use of Katō Bushi to provide the jōruri accompaniment for Sukeroku's entrance. Katō Bushi were drawn from the ranks of the wealthy merchants who were the main patrons of kabuki. When Danjūrō performs Sukeroku today, descendants of these Katō Bushi musicians provide the accompaniment.

28. Ihara, Kabuki nempyō, Vol. 2, p. 186. When Takenojō did Sukeroku in 1733, Danjūrō II played Shirozake-uri Shimbei/Soga Jūrō in the same production.
29. Ihara, Kabuki nempyō, Vol. 2, p. 304.
30. Ibid., pp. 511-12.
31. Kawatake, Nihon engeki zenshi, p. 563.
32. Nishiyama, Ichikawa Danjūrō, p. 69.

Sukeroku: Flower of Edo

As the "flower of Edo," Sukeroku was an idealized Edo townsman.[33] In traditional Japanese culture, flower is a very evocative image. While denoting natural beauty—as expressed in the youth and physical attractiveness of Sukeroku—it means much more. Most obvious is the image of the cherry blossom, the Japanese flower of flowers, which not only represented the season of spring when Sukeroku was performed,[34] but in the Tokugawa period was also the single, general symbol for the world of the theaters and gay quarters. These comprised the so-called ukiyo, or floating world, and were perfectly brought together in Sukeroku.[35] Not quite so obvious, however, are the flowers, which, manifested in Sukeroku, represented 1) the spirit of resistance of the Edo townsman—what I call Sukeroku as otokodate, and 2) the Edo townsman's attainment by virtue of wealth of the most influential position in the cultural order of Tokugawa Japan—what I call Sukeroku as fudasashi.[36]

Sukeroku as otokodate: the Spirit of Resistance

In Edo art and literature the otokodate was a champion of the people, a hero, one who, as the characters for otoko and date signify, evoked the model image of a man. He was a Robin Hood figure who helped defend the weak against the strong. He was a man of honor, chivalrous, dedicated—and he had style. He was Sukeroku.[37]

33. "Flower of Edo" applies to both Sukeroku and Danjūrō. Gunji, Kabuki to Yoshiwara, p. 65.
34. When the Sukeroku section of a long play was identified by a separate title, it usually contained a word indicating flower. For example, the title of Sukeroku in the Ichikawa family's jūhachi-ban is Sukeroku yukari no Edo-zakura. Zakura (or sakura in its unvoiced form) means cherry blossom.
35. The ukiyo was the world of beauty and impermanence, and the cherry blossom was its symbol. Cherry blossoms come every spring, but almost as soon as the long-awaited flowers begin to bloom the petals drop to the ground.
36. Flower (hana) in the case of the otokodate was primarily a metaphor for the fights that he engaged in. These fights were, of course, the expression of his resistance.
   In the case of the fudasashi, flower does not have so obvious a meaning, but if the fudasashi were the most successful merchant-townsmen, then flower, which is often used to denote completeness, is appropriate here.
37. Otokodate cannot be explained without reference to Sukeroku. Dictionaries such as Maeda Isamu, Edogo daijiten (Tokyo: Kōdansha, 1974), p. 200, refer to Sukeroku in order to define otokodate.

The real-life counterpart of the otokodate was the machi-yakko. Machi-yakko were groups of commoners who banded together in opposition to the samurai hatamoto-yakko (bannerman "fellows") in the city of Edo. While clashes between machi-yakko and hatamoto-yakko may at times have had overtones of class conflict, many of the machi-yakko were originally low-ranking samurai.[38] Unlike those hatamoto in the service of the shōgun, however, these samurai found jobs as shopkeepers, artisans, and other types of businessmen in the rapidly developing commercial sector of the city. The hatamoto, who survived on handouts in the form of rice stipends from the shōgun, were underpaid, underworked (there were no wars in which they could exercise their samurai skills) and, as a result, they formed their yakko groups which went looking for trouble in the busy streets of the city.

Care must be taken in trying to infer the significance of the fictional otokodate from the historical evidence concerning the machi-yakko. Such an attempt may lead to the following type of conclusion:

> For what reason it is not quite clear, the (machi-) yakko are credited in romantic literature with remarkable virtues. they are depicted as patterns of chivalry, and styled Otokodate. . . . It is true that some of the bands of (machi-) yakko were governed by severe codes of loyalty among themselves, and no doubt from time to time they performed quixotic acts; but . . . they seem to have been disorderly rogues and to owe their reputation chiefly to the eighteenth-century stage plays in which they figure as heroes. It is indeed a curious fact that the theater in Japan owed its development to its portrayal of these people and their exploits.[39]

The problem here is that the writer tried to make artistic works fit a limited set of historical facts, a not entirely satisfactory method of literary criticism. Moreover, the writer seems to have tried to understand Japanese culture from the point of view of his own culture and naturally, therefore, what he saw was quite "curious." If, however, we take Japan's culture as the given—and we must do this—and study the artistic works in their proper context, we find that there were good reasons why, for example, Sukeroku as otokodate became a major hero in the drama.

38. Origuchi Shinobu, "Akutai no geijutsu," in Tomita Tetsunosuke, "Sukeroku yukari no Edo-zakura: Saiken," Kikan kabuki, No. 1 (1969), 142-43.
39. George Sansom, A History of Japan, 1615-1867 (Stanford: Stanford University Press, 1963), p. 60.

The proper context for understanding the significance of Sukeroku as otokodate is the Soga tradition. Unless we keep in mind the fact that Sukeroku is Soga Gorō, Sukeroku's actions have no meaning. Sukeroku is an otokodate character precisely because he is Soga Gorō. To make this clearer, let us look at the first encounter between Sukeroku and Ikyū.

As we have seen, when Sukeroku enters the stage the courtesans all offer him a pipe. Ikyū, who is sitting nearby, does not receive a single one. When he protests, Sukeroku boldly offers him one with his foot. Ikyū is incensed and proceeds to lecture Sukeroku on what it means to be an otokodate. According to Ikyū there are five qualities that distinguish a true otokodate: righteousness, morality, courtesy, reasonableness, and a spirit of honor and pride.[40] His implication is that Sukeroku, who has achieved notoriety by fighting with all and sundry in the gay quarters[41] and behaves in such an insulting way toward him, is not an otokodate.

Sukeroku's reply is in character with the role he has assumed. He says that for him the pride of an otokodate is simply in drawing his sword on any man bold enough to resist him. And he ends by saying, "Who do you think I am? Fool!"[42] At this point Ikyū does not know who Sukeroku is and that he is actually talking to Soga Gorō. What Soga Gorō as Sukeroku is doing is all carefully planned and with purpose. The fighting and the insults are truly manifestations of righteousness and other otokodate qualities, for he is using them as ways to find the sword that will enable him to carry out the revenge. In sum, Sukeroku is an otokodate if one understands the motivation of his actions in terms of his identity as Soga Gorō.

This aspect of Sukeroku recalls the Ichiriki teahouse scene in Chūshingura, where Yuranosuke is spending his time in apparent dissipation in the gay quarters instead of working toward carrying out the revenge on Moronao.[43] Like Soga Gorō, who as Sukeroku seems to be wasting his time in the gay quarters, Yuranosuke only wants to put his enemies off their guard. The key question in both Sukeroku and Chūshingura is, as Sukeroku asks Ikyū, Dare da to omou? "Who do you think I am?"[44] Ikyū does not know, and even Sukeroku's own mother and brother are fooled.

40. Kabuki jūhachi-ban shū, ed. Gunji, p. 95.
41. There was a proverb associated with Sukeroku which went: Aite kawaredo, shu kawarazu ("Though the opponent changed, the principal was the same"), meaning that Sukeroku was always fighting, though with different people. Ibid., p. 86.
42. Ibid., p. 95.
43. Chūshingura (The Treasury of Loyal Retainers), pp. 104-24.
44. Kabuki jūhachi-ban shū, ed. Gunji, p. 95.

Given Sukeroku's identity as Soga Gorō, then, the spirit of resistance that Sukeroku as <u>otokodate</u> symbolized can be understood. In terms of the Soga tradition, it was resistance first of all against Kudō Suketsune and the powerful forces (represented by Yoritomo) that made it difficult for Gorō and Jūrō to carry out their just revenge. Going further, it was generalized resistance against all destructive and overwhelming forces. Soga Gorō was associated with the guardian diety Fudō, and was himself a god-hero—becoming so by means of the aragoto art of Danjūrō I.[45]

Sukeroku was a hero in the same tradition as Soga Gorō. Sukeroku, however, was of the new order while Soga Gorō was of the old order. Sukeroku was a pure Edo figure—in essence, a contemporary manifestation of Soga Gorō. The forces he represented resistance against included not only the political forces of the Tokugawa period, but also evil "forces" such as fire, earthquake, business uncertainty—all of them contemporary problems. Life in the Tokugawa period was uncertain. Earthquake and fire[46] were constantly threatening and frequently destructive, and business, which was just developing on a full scale in Edo, was often risky. Just as their forefathers did, the people of the Tokugawa period turned to their heroes, their gods, to protect them against the uncertainties and to give them the power and strength that they themselves did not otherwise have.[47]

What are the elements that are evidence of the spirit of resistance of Sukeroku as <u>otokodate</u>? They may be divided into three categories: 1) action, 2) costume and make-up, and 3) speech. Sukeroku's actions are those of the aragoto hero, but they are actions appropriate to a hero of the modern city of Edo—not to a warrior from a previous age like Soga Gorō. Sukeroku's posture is always assertive, yet elegant. His dance entrance on the hanamachi, which is a series of assertive poses done with the assistance of his snake's eye umbrella, is a good example of this. In the course of the play, Sukeroku engages in a number of fight scenes with Ikyū and his men, and always emerges calmly as the winner.

Sukeroku's costume and make-up are also those of an aggressive hero. Most outstanding are the <u>kenka no hachimaki</u> ("fight headband") and the <u>kumadori</u> make-up. Not only does the headband identify its wearer as an

---

45. Aragoto was in itself an expression of resistance. Tomita, "<u>Sukeroku yukari no Edo-zakura: Saiken</u>," 133.
46. There was, for example, the Meireki fire of 1657, in which more than half of Edo was destroyed. See Sansom, <u>A History of Japan, 1615-1867</u>, pp. 61-62.
47. Nishiyama and Takeuchi, <u>Edo</u>, p. 32.

aragoto hero, but its purple color also signifies "abiding ties"[48]—the ties of love (toward Agemaki) and the ties of duty to his family and to the revenge. Sukeroku's mukimi style of kumadori, which is the principal visual feature of the aragoto hero, is especially noteworthy since it is the same as that of Soga Gorō.[49] Thus, the make-up makes clear the association between the two characters.[50]

Finally, Sukeroku's speech provides the finest examples of his spirit of resistance. The style of speech is called akutai, and is characterized by barrages of insults delivered in a rapid-fire manner. The best instance is Sukeroku's introduction of himself, quoted earlier in the summary of the play. Other instances are when Sukeroku says:

> reason with a wise man, but kick a mule in the ass. I deflate the pompous braggard with a touch of my clog.[51]

> Blockhead! Beanpaste brain! Outhouse ass![52]

There are even times when Sukeroku will use meaningless syllables just because they sound menacing. "Yattoko, totcha" is a good example.[53]

In all, Sukeroku's actions, costume, make-up, and speech established him as the ultimate Edokko—that special class of Edo townsman, born and bred in Edo, and, most important of all, characterized by iki and hari—the spirit of resistance.[54] Scholars do not seem to be able to say enough about Sukeroku and the idea of resistance. Toita Yasuji sums it up by simply labeling Sukeroku "the champion of the Edokko."[55]

Sukeroku as Fudasashi: a Change in the View of Sukeroku as Otokodate

As the career of Danjūrō II matured and as the position of the townsman in Edo became more stable and secure, the image of Sukeroku as

---

48. "Sukeroku: Flower of Edo," p. 63. The chorus sings: "A headband such as this one in times long ago; spoke through its purple color of abiding ties."
49. Toita, Kabuki jūhachi-ban, p. 114.
50. Toita emphasizes that since Sukeroku was really Soga Gorō, it was only natural that their style of make-up be the same. Ibid., p. 115.
51. "Sukeroku: Flower of Edo," p. 66.
52. Ibid., p. 72.
53. Ibid.
54. Edo, ed. Kasai Harunobu (Tokyo: Yomiuri Shimbun Sha, 1978), pp. 129-30.
55. Toita, Kabuki jūhachi-ban, p. 119.

otokodate was modified to one of Sukeroku as fudasashi. This was not so much a break with past practice as it was a refinement of it. Sukeroku as otokodate had been a hero of resistance; Sukeroku as fudasashi was still a hero of resistance, but one who had reached the pinnacle of success. By the mid-eighteenth century, the economic success of the townsmen of Edo had enabled them to establish themselves as the cultural leaders of their age. The samurai may have occupied first place in the official hierarchy, but the wealthy merchants, and especially the fudasashi, had the real power and influence in "popular" society.

Proof of this modified view of Sukeroku is that at the time of Danjūrō II's third Sukeroku, Sukeroku was modeled on Oguchiya Gyou, a leading Edo fudasashi, one of the so-called daihachi daitsū—the eight great townsman-merchant Edokko.[56] Moreover, by this time Katō Bushi musicians, who were fudasashi by occupation, were providing the accompaniment for Sukeroku's important dance entrance.[57] In kabuki, where there is usually no place for non-professional performers, the presence of the amateur Katō Bushi was evidence of the close association between Sukeroku and the fudasashi.

Since the fudasashi were major patrons of kabuki, Sukeroku as fudasashi may be viewed not only as a statement of townsman success, but also as the theater's way of thanking these townsmen for their patronage and support. This can be seen in the selection of Oguchiya Gyou as the model for Danjūrō II's third Sukeroku. Other evidence is a drawing by Utagawa Toyokuni in E-hon shibai nenjū-kagami showing the actors who played the roles of Sukeroku and Agemaki, accompanied by the teahouse managers whose business depended on the theaters, making formal rounds of greetings to their patrons.

In sum, Sukeroku as fudasashi was an exaltation of the townsmen of the kabuki audience. Edo kabuki was a mirror of the success that the Edo townsmen had achieved and Danjūrō's portrayal of Sukeroku was the image they saw in that mirror. In works such as Edo murasaki hiiki no hachimaki (1810), (Hana no Edo) Kabuki nendaiki (the titles of which are explicit references to Danjūrō and Sukeroku),[58] and in assorted prints, we see testimonies to Edo itself. The kabuki theater, after all, was where so many of the energies of Edo converged.

56. Kawatake, Nihon engeki zenshi, p. 515.
57. Toita, Kabuki jūhachi-ban, pp. 104, 118.
58. Tachikawa Emba, Edo murasaki hiiki no hachimaki. Manuscript owned by Waseda University's Engeki Hakubutsukan. Murasaki (purple) and hachimaki (headband) refer, of course, to Sukeroku's purple headband (which Danjūrō wore in the role). Hana no Edo ("Edo the flower") in Tachikawa, Hana no Edo Kabuki nendaiki means both Sukeroku and Danjūrō.

Sukeroku as <u>fudasashi</u> was the final step in the evolution of the
Sukeroku inoovation within the Soga traditional framework.   Except for
parodies in the nineteenth century,[59] this view of Sukeroku has remained the
same.

59. An example is <u>Kurodegumi kuruwa no tatehiki</u> by Kawatake Mokuami.

CONCLUSION

The meaning of Sukeroku's double identity emerges from a dramatic structure set within the framework of the traditional calendar of kabuki. Soga Gorō, the samurai god-hero of the first months of the spring production, was transformed into Sukeroku, the townsman of the latter months of the production. This change within the cycle was a movement from the realm of the old order to the realm of the new order. The double identity served as a structural link between the two realms.

Even to appreciate what remains of kabuki today, we must understand the nature of Tokugawa-period kabuki. It was based primarily on a cyclical pattern, one that was an outgrowth of the singularly intimate relationship in Japanese culture between artistic structure and seasonal rhythms. Long after major urban centers had been established and townsmen were generations removed from the actual experience of agricultural life (which had given rise to the prototypical cycle), novels, poems, and plays were made according to a pattern of seasonal movement. Of course, kabuki also accommodated a non-cyclical or linear time. This represented the accumulation of tradition—which has an important role not only in kabuki, but in all Japanese classical art forms. The tradition of Soga plays was established in the early dramatic forms of nō, kōwaka, and ko-jōruri and came to occupy a major place in kabuki. To keep traditions alive, playwrights used various types of innovations, an example of which is the joining of Sukeroku to the Soga framework.

Once kabuki is seen in terms of its traditional calendar and the principles of tradition and innovation, the meaning of "a play" becomes clear. "A play" such as Sukeroku was not a single, complete work, but one section of the calendar as a whole. Moreover, "a play" in kabuki was not a finished product but part of a continuing process wherein every production differed from, but recalled, earlier productions. Thus, it was not until late in the history of kabuki (starting near the end of the eighteenth century) that "definitive" texts were preserved, which thereby removed a work from the

process of change. It is at that point that we begin to refer to kabuki as
classic.

Seen from the perspective of its calendar, kabuki was neither illogical
nor incoherent, as some have suggested. Rather, it was an extended,
intricately bound structure built on the rhythms of the changing year. Take
away that idea of cycle and the structure becomes fragmented, unintelligible.

The very logic of kabuki is perfectly revealed in the double identity of
Soga Gorō and Sukeroku. It was the nature of kabuki to strike a harmonious
balance between time present and time past. When audiences saw Danjūrō as
Sukeroku, they saw the present in its most vital form, as the springtime, as
the flower of Edo. At the same time they saw Danjūrō as Soga Gorō, who
represented the power and dignity of the past. In Japanese culture, the past
lives on in the present; Soga Gorō was a god-hero and the logic of kabuki
enabled Sukeroku, the courtesan's idol, to appear as his contemporary
manifestation.

Postscript

RECONSTRUCTING KABUKI FOR PERFORMANCE

As a postscript to this book, I would like to say a few words about the attempt by Japan's National Theater, the Kokuritsu Gekijō, to reconstruct kabuki for actual presentation on stage.

The National Theater opened in November 1966 with the aim of providing a center for the study and performance of the traditional arts, especially kabuki and the puppet theater of bunraku, or ningyō-jōruri. As supporters of the project saw it, the most exciting undertaking of the new theater, and the feature that promised to make it unique among existing theaters, was the production of kabuki in its "original classical form," as reconstructed tōshi-kyōgen.[1]

The first presentation of the new theater was the tōshi-kyōgen version of Sugawara denju tenarai kagami, which is regarded as one of the three most popular plays in the kabuki repertory (along with Yoshitsune sembon-zakara and Chūshingura). Because the length of time required to do the whole work was approximately twelve hours, and because modern audiences do not have the time nor the desire to spend an entire day at the theater, it was decided to produce only the first half one month and to do the rest the following month. After that the practice of dividing extremely long works into two parts and presenting them in consecutive months became usual in National Theater productions.

When Sugawara was produced in November and December 1966, audiences were able to see sections of the play that had not been performed in decades—such as the daijo, or prologue—along with sections that are seen quite often, such as Kuruma-biki and Terakoya. In January 1967, when Narukami Fudō Kitayama-zakura was produced as the second work of the new

1. Teranaka Sakuo, "Operation and projects of the National Theater," in National Theater of Japan, translated by Kimura Kimi and Karashima Atsumi (Tokyo: Kokuritsu Gekijō, 1970), p. 12.

theater, the <u>Kenuki,</u> <u>Narukami,</u> and <u>Fudō</u> sections were given in the same production as they had two hundred and twenty-five years before.[2] Although the practice of reconstructing plays became well established at the National Theater, it has not been accepted without criticism by theatergoers and actors alike.

A review of the opening of the very first production is representative. The critic found that although the production was "faithful to the original" (<u>koten ni chūjitsu</u>), the "kabuki feeling" was somehow lacking.[3] The tremendous amount of research that went into the reconstruction of plays made the production of kabuki at the National Theater seem pedantic. Later, some commentators suggested that a solution lay in investing more time, money and talent into each production.[4] This made kabuki at the National Theater extraordinarily lavish, both scenically and in the amount of historical detail, but it still left many dissatisfied. As Onoe Baikō, a top actor who has frequently played leading roles in National Theater productions, said about the reconstruction of kabuki: "If, over a long period of time, our predecessors dropped certain plays and sections of plays from the repertory, they had their reasons."[5]

Their reasons, of course, derived from the way kabuki was structured during the Tokugawa period, which was not sufficiently taken into account in the new productions. On the one hand, the National Theater had assumed that the parts of plays which had been produced independently for decades, even centuries, could and, moreover, should be returned to some sort of original context. And, on the other hand, it had been thought that plays from which parts had been taken could be easily reconstructed; it was only a matter of research and reworking to put things back together. But, of course, kabuki was based on relatively short, potentially independent dramatic units that could be moved from context to context or taken out of the repertory altogether. Because of this the problem of balance in the plays was naturally the most difficult obstacle to overcome. Some sections had become so self-sufficient from performance "out of context" that they resisted being put back in with other sections that had been long neglected. This could have an adverse effect on both actors and audience when it was felt that parts of a

2. See <u>Kabuki: Five Classic Plays</u>, pp. 95-97.
3. Akiyama Yasusaburō, "Koten ni chūjitsu da ga 'usuaji,'" <u>Asahi Shimbun, Yūkan,</u> 12 November 1966, p. 12.
4. "Tōshi-kyōgen ni genkai-setsu," <u>Asahi Shimbun, Yūkan,</u> 26 November 1970, p. 9.
5. <u>Ibid.</u>

play had to be done just for the sake of the idea that everything should be done.

Another assumption was that any play in the repertory could be reconstructed. In practice, however, as Gunji has pointed out, this concept applies for the most part to jōruri-derived kabuki and kabuki in a similar structural tradition (mainly Kamigata kabuki), and not to Edo kabuki—that is, kabuki in the tradition of Danjūrō, which includes Sukeroku.[6]

Gunji observes that, looking back over the years that the National Theater has been in operation, the emphasis has been on plays such as Sugawara denju tenarai kagami, Yoshitsune sembon-zakara, and Chūshingura—all derived from the jōruri theater. He argues that the structure of these plays appears "modern" and "logical," while the structure of Edo kabuki embodies features—such as double identities—that today's society will only find illogical. Of course, Edo kabuki was not illogical but was based on a performance calendar which provided the controlling context for each play that was produced in the course of it.

6. Gunji, Namari to suigin, p. 95.

SELECT BIBLIOGRAPHY

Akiba Yoshimi. "Keihan no Sukeroku kogyō nempyō." Engei gekkan, February 1930, pp. 1-7.

Akiyama Yasusaburō. "Koten ni chūjitsu da ga 'usuaji.'" Asahi Shimbun, Yūkan, 12 November 1966, p. 12.

Andō Tōan. "Yōkyoku oyobi kōwaka-mai no Soga-mono." Yōkyoku-kai, 10, No. 6 (1919), 37-48.

Anesaki Masaharu. History of Japanese Religion. London: Kegan Paul, Trench, Trubner, 1930.

Araki, James T. The Ballad Drama of Medieval Japan. Berkeley: University of California Press, 1964.

Atsumi Seitarō. Kabuki nyūmon. Tokyo: Tōkai Shobō, 1949.

_____. "Sekai to tōjō-jimbutsu." In Kabuki zensho, Ed. Toita Yasuji. Tokyo: Sōgensha, 1956, II, 53-95.

_____. "Soga kyōgen no hensen to kanshō." Engeki-kai, 8, No. 2 (1950), 11-19.

_____. "Sukeroku nendaiki." Engei gahō, June 1930, pp. 30-35.

_____. "Sukeroku no yurai". Engei gahō, March 1925; reprinted in (Kokuritsu Gekijō) Jōen shiryō shū, No. 134 (January 1977), pp. 34-66.

Benedict, Ruth. The Chrysanthemum and the Sword, Patterns of Japanese Culture. Boston: Houghton Mifflin, 1946.

Blacker, Carmen. The Catalpa Bow: A Study of Shamanistic Practices in Japan. London: George Allen and Unwin, 1975.

Brandon, James R., William P. Malm, and Donald H. Shively. Studies in Kabuki: Its Acting, Music and Historical Context. Honolulu: The University Press of Hawaii, 1978.

Brustein, Robert. "Drama in the Age of Einstein." New York Times, 7 August
    1977, Sec. 2, pp. 1,22.

Chūshingura (The Treasury of Loyal Retainers). Trans. Donald Keene. New
    York: Columbia University Press, 1971.

Daigo Yoshiyasu. Kigo jiten. Tokyo: Tōkyōdō, 1968.

Edo. Ed. Kasai Harunobu. Tokyo: Yomiuri Shimbun Sha, 1978.

Engi-Shiki: Procedures of the Engi Era. Trans. Felicia Gressitt Bock.
    Tokyo: Sophia University, 1970. Vol. I.

Ernst, Earle. The Kabuki Theatre. 1956; rpt. Honolulu: The University Press
    of Hawaii, 1974.

Fukuzawa Yukichi. The Autobiography of Fukuzawa Yukichi. Rev. trans. by
    Eiichi Kiyooka. New York: Shocken Books, 1966.

Genroku kabuki kessaku shū.   Ed. Takano Tatsuyuki and Kuroki Kanzō.
    Tokyo: Waseda Daigaku Shuppan-bu, 1925. Vol. I.

Gentles, Margaret. Masters of the Japanese Print: Moronobu to Utamaro.
    New York: The Asia Society, 1964.

Gondō Yoshikazu. Nō no mikata. Kyoto: Tōyō Bunka Sha, 1975.

Gunji Masakatsu. "Aragoto no seiritsu." In his Kabuki: yōshiki to denshō, pp.
    15-32.

_____. "Aragoto no sekai." Kikan kabuki, bessatsu, No. 1 (Sept. 1969),
    pp. 102-23.

_____. Kabuki. In Iwanami Kōza: Nihon bungaku shi, Vol. VIII,
    Kinsei. Tokyo: Iwanami Shoten, 1958.

_____. Kabuki. Trans. John Bester. Palo Alto: Kodansha, 1969.

_____. Kabuki fukuro. Tokyo: Seiabō, 1970.

_____. "Kabuki kyakuhon no hensen." In Kabuki techō. Ed. Toita
    Yasuji. Osaka: Sōgensha, 1951, pp. 42-59.

_____. Kabuki no bigaku. Tokyo: Engeki Shuppansha, 1975.

_____. Kabuki no hassō. Tokyo: Kōbundō, 1959.

_____. Kabuki nyūmon. New ed. Tokyo: Shakai Shisō Kenkyūkai Shuppanbu, 1962.

_____. Kabuki to Yoshiwara. Tokyo: Awaji Shobō, 1956.

_____. Kabuki: yōshiki to denshō. Tokyo: Gakugei Shorin, 1969.

_____. Namari to suigin. Tokyo: Nishizawa Shoten, 1975.

_____. "Soga monogatari to Soga kyōgen." Engeki-kai, 8, No. 2 (1950), 5-10.

Haikai and Haiku. Ed. Ichikawa Sanki, et al. Tokyo: Nippon Gakujutsu Shinkōkai, 1958.

Halford, Aubrey S. and Giovanna M. The Kabuki Handbook. Rutland, Vt.: Charles E. Tuttle, 1956.

Hattori Yukio. Hengeron: Kabuki no seishin-shi. Tokyo: Heibonsha, 1975.

_____. "Kabuki: Kōzō no keisei." In Kabuki. Vol. VIII of Nihon no koten geinō. Ed. Geinō-shi Kenkyūkai. Tokyo: Heibonsha, 1971, pp. 7-85.

_____. Kabuki no genzō. Tokyo: Asuka Shobō, 1974.

_____. Kabuki no kōzō. Tokyo: Chūō Kōron Sha, 1970.

_____. Kabuki seiritsu no kenkyū. Tokyo: Kazama Shobō, 1968.

Hayashiya Tatsusaburō. Kabuki izen. Tokyo: Iwanami Shoten, 1954.

Hibbett, Howard S. "The Japanese Comic Linked-Verse Tradition" Harvard Journal of Asiatic Studies, 23 (1960-61), 76-92.

Hirosue Tamotsu. Akubasho no hassō. Tokyo: Sanseidō, 1970.

Hori Ichirō. Folk Religion in Japan: Continuity and Change. Ed. Joseph M. Kitagawa and Alan L. Miller. Chicago: University of Chicago Press, 1968.

Ihara Saikaku. Five Women Who Loved Love. Trans. Wm. Theodore deBary. Rutland, Vt.: Charles E. Tuttle, 1956.

_____. The Japanese Family Storehouse. Trans. G. W. Sargent. Cambridge: Cambridge University Press, 1959.

_____. Worldly Mental Calculations: An Annotated Translation of Ihara Saikaku's Seken munezan'yō. Trans. Ben Befu. Berkeley: University of California Press, 1976.

Ihara Toshirō. Danjūrō no shibai. Tokyo: Waseda Daigaku Shuppan-bu, 1934.

_____. Kabuki nempyō. 8 vols. Tokyo: Iwanami Shoten, 1956.

_____. "Kyōgen no hensen." Waseda bungaku, July 1895, 361-72.

_____. "Tsuzuki-kyōgen okorite yori irai no gigei." Waseda bungaku, December 1895, 905-23.

Iizuka Tomoichirō. Kabuki gairon. Tokyo: Hakubunkan, 1928.

_____. Kabuki saiken. Tokyo: Daiichi Shobō, 1927.

Imao Tetsuya. Henshin no shisō. Tokyo: Hōsei Daigaku Shuppan-kyoku, 1970.

Inoura Yoshinobu. A History of Japanese Theater I: Up to Noh and Kyogen. Tokyo: Kokusai Bunka Shinkōkai, 1971.

Jaynes, Julian. The Origin of Consciousness in the Breakdown of the Bicameral Mind. Boston: Houghton Mifflin, 1977.

Kabuki: Five Classic Plays. Trans. James R. Brandon. Cambridge, Mass.: Harvard University Press, 1975.

Kabuki hyōbanki shūsei. Ed. Kabuki Hyōbanki Kenkyūkai. 11 vols. Tokyo: Iwanami Shoten, 1972-77.

Kabuki jūhachi-ban shū. Ed. Gunji Masakatsu. Nihon koten bungaku taikei, 98. Tokyo: Iwanami Shoten, 1965.

Kabuki kyakuhon shū. Ed. Urayama Masao and Matsuzaki Hitoshi. 2 vols. Nihon koten bungaku taikei, 53 & 54. Tokyo: Iwanami Shoten, 1961.

Kageyama Haruki. The Arts of Shinto. Trans. and adapt. by Christine Guth. New York: Weatherhill, 1973.

Kawatake Shigetoshi. "Gikyoku no rekishi." In Kabuki zensho, II, 3-52.

_____. Kabuki hyakudai. Tokyo: Seiabō, 1959.

_____. Kabuki-shi no kenkyū. Tokyo: Tōkyōdō, 1943.

_____. Nihon engeki zenshi. Tokyo: Iwanami Shoten, 1959.

_____. Nihon gikyoku-shi. Tokyo: Nan'undō Ofūsha, 1964.

Kawatake Shigetoshi Hakase Kiju Kinen Shuppan Kankōkai. Nihon engeki kenkyū shomoku kaidai. Tokyo: Heibonsha, 1970.

Keene, Donald. World Within Walls. New York: Holt, Rinehart, and Winston, 1976.

Kezairoku. 1801; rpt. in Kinsei geidō-ron. Ed. Nishiyama Matsunosuke, et al. Nihon shisō taikei, 61. Tokyo: Iwanami Shoten, 1972, pp. 493-532.

Kikan hōgaku. No. 7 (April 1976). Special issue on Sambasō.

Kobayashi Shizuo. "Soga monogatari to kusemai." Koten kenkyū, 6, No. 4 (1941), 96-101.

Ko-jōruri shōhon shū. Ed. Yokoyama Shigeru. Tokyo: Kadokawa Shoten, 1964. Vol. II.

Kokugeki yōran. Ed. Engeki Hakubutsukan. Tokyo: Azusa Shobō, 1932.

Konishi Jin'ichi. "Association and Progression: Principles of Integration in Anthologies and Sequences of Japanese Court Poetry, A.D. 900-1350." Trans. and adapt. by Robert H. Brower and Earl Miner. Harvard Journal of Asiatic Studies, 21 (1958), 67-127.

Maeda Isamu. Edogo daijiten. Tokyo: Kōdansha, 1974.

Matsunaga, Alicia. The Buddhist Philosophy of Assimilation: The Historical Development of the Honji-suijaku Theory. Rutland, Vt.: Charles E. Tuttle, 1969.

Matsuzaki Hitoshi. "Kabuki kyōgen no kōzō." Kokubungaku kaishaku to kyōzai no kenkyū, 20, No. 8 (1975), 52-59.

Mimasuya Nisōji. Sakusha nenjū-gyōji. 1852; rpt. in Kabuki, Vol. VI of Nihon shomin bunka shiryō shūsei, Tokyo: San'ichi Shobō, 1973, pp. 669-715.

Miner, Earl. Japanese Linked Poetry, An Account with Translations of Renga
and Haikai Sequences. Princeton: Princeton University Press, 1979.

Miyamasu. "Chōbuku Soga: A Noh Play by Miyamasu." Trans. Laurence
Bresler. Monumenta Nipponica, 29, No. 1 (1974), 69–81.

_____. "The Noh as Popular Theater: Miyamasu's Youchi Soga."
Trans. Laurence Kominz. Monumenta Nipponica, 33, No. 4 (1978), 441–
59.

Moriyama Shigeo. "Geki no seiritsu to geki no shisō: Soga-mono ni tsuite."
Bungaku, 32, No. 7 (1964), 725–36.

Muroki Yatarō. Katarimono (mai, sekkyō, kojōruri) no kenkyū. Tokyo:
Kazama Shobō, 1970.

Nakamura Kichizō. Nihon gikyoku gikō-ron. Tokyo: Chūō Kōron Sha, 1942.

Nakamura Yukihiko. Gesaku-ron. Tokyo: Kadokawa Shoten, 1966.

_____. "Kabuki no shukō to asobi no seishin." Program of the
Kokuritsu Gekijō, Tokyo. Sept. 1965, pp. 30–31.

_____. "Modes of Expression in a Historical Context." Acta Asiatica,
28 (1975), 1–19.

Nishiyama Matsunosuke. Edo chōnin no kenkyū. 3 vols. Tokyo: Yoshikawa
Kōbunkan, 1972–73.

_____. Ichikawa Danjūrō. Tokyo: Yoshikawa Kōbunkan, 1960.

_____ and Takeuchi Makoto. Edo. Vol. II. Vol. V of Edo jidai zushi.
Tokyo: Chikuma Shobō, 1976.

Okazaki Yoshie. "Genroku kabuki no sekai kōzō." In his Nihon bungeigaku.
Tokyo: Iwanami Shoten, 1935, pp. 334–64.

Origuchi Shinobu. "Akutai no geijutsu." In Tomita Tetsunosuke, "Sukeroku
yukari no Edo-zakura: Saiken," Kikan kabuki, No. 1 (1969), 142–43.

Ruch, Barbara. "Medieval Jongleurs and the Making of a National
Literature." In Japan in the Muromachi Age. Ed. John Whitney Hall and
Toyoda Takeshi. Berkeley: Univ. of California Press, 1977, pp. 279–309.

Sakamoto Setchō. "Soga monogatari to yōkyoku." Nōgaku, 2, No. 6 (1951), 2-12, and No. 7, 2-13.

Sansom, George. A History of Japan, 1615-1867. Stanford: Stanford Univ. Press, 1963.

Santo Kyōden. Sukeroku kyōgen-kō. In Kinsei kiseki-kō, 1804; reprinted in Nihon zuihitsu zenshu, Tokyo: Kokumin Tosho, 1929, XI, 125-28.

Sei Shōnagon. The Pillow Book of Sei Shonagon. Trans. and ed. Ivan Morris. Baltimore: Penguin Books, 1971.

Sekai kōmoku. Reprinted in Kyōgen sakusha shiryō-shū (1): Sekai kōmoku, Shibai nenjū-gyōji. Tokyo: Kokuritsu Gekijō, 1974, pp. 7-84.

Shimazu Hisamoto. "Kōwaka no Soga-mono." Kokugo to kokubungaku, 10, No. 4 (1933), 111-22.

Shively, Donald H. "Bakufu versus Kabuki." Harvard Journal of Asiatic Studies, 18 (1955), 326-56.

Shōkadō Hajō. Shibai nenjū-gyōji, 1777; rpt. in Kyōgen sakusha shiryō-shū (1): Sekai kōmoku, Shibai nenjū-gyōji, pp. 85-96.

Shuzui Kenji. Kabuki-geki gikyoku kōzō no kenkyū. Tokyo: Hokuryūkan, 1947.

_____. "Kinsei engeki gaisetsu." Kokugo to kokubungaku, No. 414, (Oct. 1958), pp. 1-15.

_____. Kinsei gikyoku kenkyū. Tokyo: Chūkōkan, 1932.

_____ and Akiba Yoshimi. Kabuki zusetsu. Tokyo: Chūbunkan Shoten, 1932-33.

Soga kyōgen gappei-shū. Ed. Atsumi Seitarō. Vol. XIV of Nihon gikyoku zenshū. Tokyo: Shun'yōdō, 1929.

Soga monogatari. Ed. Ichiko Teiji and Oshima Tatehiko. Nihon koten bungaku taikei, 88. Tokyo: Iwanami Shoten, 1966.

"Sukeroku: Flower of Edo." In Kabuki: Five Classic Plays, pp. 49-92.

Sukeroku kenkyū shiryō. Tokyo: Zenshin-za, 1958.

Suwa Haruo. Genroku kabuki no kenkyū. Tokyo: Kasama Shoin, 1967.

Suzuki Eisuke. "Wakashu kabuki no monomane kyōgen." In Engeki-shi kenkyū. Ed. Tokyo Teidai Engeki-shi Gakkai. Tokyo: Daiichi Shobō, 1932. Vol. II, 124-30.

Tachikawa Emba. Edo murasaki hiiki no hachimaki. 1810. Manuscript owned by Waseda Daigaku Engeki Hakubutsukan.

_____. (Hana no Edo) Kabuki nendaiki. 1815; rpt. Tokyo: Ōtori Shuppan, 1976.

Takamura Chikuri. E-hon shibai nenjū-kagami. 1803; rpt. in Shibai nenjū-gyōji shū, Tokyo: Kokuritsu Gekijō, 1976, pp. 185-241.

Takano Masami. Kinsei engeki no kenkyū. Tokyo: Tōkyōdō, 1941.

Takano Tatsuyuki. Nihon engeki-shi. Tokyo: Tōkyōdō, 1948. Vol. II.

Takaoka Nobuyuki. "Soga no taimen zakkan." Engeki-kai, 16, No. 1 (1958), 29-32.

Takaya, Ted. "An Inquiry into the Role of the Traditional Kabuki Playwright." Dissertation, Columbia University, 1969.

Tamenaga Itchō. Kabuki jishi. 1762; rpt. in Kabuki, Vol. VI of Nihon shomin bunka shiryō shūsei, pp. 87-133.

Tanaka Makoto. "Soga-mono yōkyoku ni tsuite." Hōsei, 19, No. 11 (1943), 69-73.

_____. "Yōkyoku no haikyoku." In Nō-gaku zensho. Ed. Nogami Toyoichirō. Tokyo: Sōgensha, 1942, Vol. III, 337-80.

Teranaka Sakuo. "Operation and projects of the National Theatre." In National Theatre of Japan. Trans. Kimura Kimi and Karashima Atsumi. Tokyo: Kokuritsu Gekijō, 1970.

Togi Masatarō. Gagaku: Court Music and Dance. Trans. Don Kenny. New York: Walker/Weatherhill, 1971.

Toita Yasuji. Kabuki jūhachi-ban. Tokyo: Chūō Kōron Sha, 1969.

_____. "Soga kyōgen." In his Kabuki daijesuto. Tokyo: Kurashi no Techō Sha, 1934, pp. 109-24.

"Tōshi-kyōgen ni genkai-setsu." Asahi Shimbun, Yūkan, 26 November 1970, p. 9.

Umehara Takeshi. "The Genealogy of Avenging Spirits." Trans. Susanna Contini. Diogenes, No. 84 (1974), 17-30.

Urayama Masao. "Naimaze to sekai." In Geinō no kagaku. Vol. V of Geinō ronkō, II. Ed. Tokyo Kokuritsu Bunkazai Kenkyūjo Geinōbu. Tokyo: Heibonsha, 1974, pp. 103-20.

Waseda Daigaku Engeki Hakubutsukan. Engeki hyakka daijiten. 6 vols. Tokyo: Heibonsha, 1966.

Watsuji Tetsurō. Nihon geijutsu-shi kenkyū: Kabuki to ayatsuri-jōruri. Tokyo: Iwanami Shoten, 1971.

Yakusha irokeizu. In Kabuki hyōbanki shūsei. Ed. Kabuki Hyōbanki Kenkyūkai. Tokyo: Iwanami Shoten, 1974. Vol. V, 353-465.

Yakusha mannenreki. In Kabuki hyōbanki shūsei. Vol. II, 471-592.

Yamaguchi Gō. "Sukeroku no seiritsu to sono henkei." Kabuki kenkyū. Part I: No. 7 (1926), pp. 146-59; Part II: No. 8 (1926), pp. 222-40.

Yamamoto Jirō, Kikuchi Akira, and Hayashi Kyōhei. Kabuki jiten. Tokyo: Jitsugyō no Nihon Sha, 1972.

Yoshida Kenkō. Essays in Idleness: The Tsurezuregusa of Kenko. Trans. Donald Keene. New York: Columbia University Press, 1967.

Yoshida Teruji. "Gashū Sukeroku." Kikan kabuki bessatsu, No. 1 (September 1969), 188-95.

APPENDIX I

Kabuki Source Materials of the Tokugawa Period

The most important types of kabuki source materials of the Tokugawa period for this study were critiques of actors and performances (hyōbanki), chronologies (nendaiki and nempyō), playbills (banzuke), and writings on theatrical matters (gekisho).

Critiques of kabuki actors and performances in the cities of Edo, Kyoto, and Osaka were published annually from the middle of the seventeenth century to the end of the Tokugawa period. Although they focus on acting technique rather than on the dramatic content of the plays, they were useful (especially in the case of Danjūrō II's Sukeroku) for finding information on the productions.

Chronologies are invaluable year-by-year listings of what was produced in each major theater throughout the Tokugawa period. The most useful ones were Tachikawa Emba's (Hana no Edo) Kabuki nendaiki, which, in addition to its annual listings, also contains illustrations and occasional comments on plays and players, and Ihara Toshirō's Kabuki nempyō, which was compiled from material contained in works dating from the Tokugawa period.

Playbills either advertised plays in advance of their opening or were handed out at theaters, teahouses, and bookshops at the time of performance. Their function was the same as that of posters, handbills, and theater programs today. Because texts are not available for many plays of the Tokugawa period, certain playbills (especially those of the e-hon, or "picture book," variety, which contain summaries of plays) were helpful in assessing the contents and dramatic form of plays. Many playbills have been reproduced by Shuzui Kenji in Kabuki zusetsu.

Writings on theatrical matters cover a variety of topics and range in style from historical to theoretical. The best ones for my purposes were the Kezairoku, the Sekai kōmoku, and the works on the traditional performance calendar. I also used a number of items included in the sixth volume (Kabuki) of <u>Nihon shomin bunka shiryō shūsei</u>, which is a collection of reprints of writings on theatrical matters.

In listing kabuki source materials of the Tokugawa period, I cannot omit to mention prints. Some are the work of prominent artists, who made them either to illustrate writings of the sort that are mentioned above, or made them as independent works of art.

APPENDIX II

List of Japanese Terms, Names, and Titles

Abura-uri Shimbei	油売新兵衛
Agemaki	揚巻
ageya	揚げ屋
Aigo	愛護
Aizen Soga	あいぜんそが
akutai	悪態
aragoto	荒事
aragyō	荒行
ara-hito-gami	荒人神
Araki Saemon	荒木左衛門
Araki Yojibei-za	荒木与次兵衛座
ara-mitama	荒御魂
Asagao Sembei	朝顔仙平
Asahina	朝比奈
Asano	浅野
ato o dasu	後を出す
Azuma kagami	吾妻鏡
bandachi	番立
banzuke	番付け
Benkei	弁慶
bon	盆
Chikamatsu Monzaemon	近松門左衛門
Chōbuku Soga	調伏曾我
chōnin	町人
Chūjō Hime	中将姫
Chūjō Hime kyō-hina	中将姫京雛
Chūshingura	忠臣蔵
Daidōji Tahatanosuke	大道寺田畑之助
daihachi daitsū	大八大通
daijo	大序

91

<u>Dainihon tekkai sennin</u>	大日本鉄界仙人
dampen-teki	断片的
doyō	土用
doyō-yasumi	土用休み
Dōzaburō	団三郎
Edo Handayū Bushi	江戸半太夫節
<u>Edo murasaki kongen Soga</u>	江戸紫根元曾我
Edo no sanza	江戸の三座
e-iri kyōgen bon	絵入り狂言本
En'ya Hangan	塩治判官
fudasashi	札差
Fudō Myōō	不動明王
Fujimoto Tobun	藤本斗文
<u>Fukubiki Soga</u>	福引そが
Fukui Yagozaemon	福井弥五左衛門
<u>Fukujin-asobi</u>	福神遊
futa-tateme	二立目
gekisho	劇書
gembuku	元服
<u>Gembuku Soga</u>	元服曾我
<u>Gempeigun</u>	源平軍
<u>Gempuku Soga</u> (see <u>Gembuku Soga</u>)	
<u>Gikeiki</u>	義経記
goryō	御霊
<u>Gosan</u>	御傘
goze	瞽女
<u>Hanafusa bunshin Soga</u>	英分身曾我
Hanakawado no Sukeroku	花川戸の助六
hanare-kyōgen	放れ狂言
<u>Hana-yakata Aigo no waka</u>	花館愛護若
<u>Hana-yakata Aigo-zakura</u>	花屋形愛護桜
Hanshichi	半七
hari	張り
haru kyōgen	春狂言
hatamoto-yakko	旗本奴
hatsu-haru kyōgen	初春狂言
<u>Hatsumotoyui kayoi Soga</u>	初䯰通曾我
hatsu-uma	初午
<u>Heike monogatari</u>	平家物語
hentai kambun	変体漢文
<u>Hinin no kataki-uchi</u>	非人の敵討

Hirai Yasumasa	平井保昌
Hisamatsu	久松
hito-gami	人神
honji-suijaku	本地垂迹
hyōbanki	評判記
ichi-bamme kyōgen	一番目狂言
ichidai issei	一代一世
Ichikawa Danjūrō	市川団十郎
Ichikawa Kuzō	市川九蔵
Ichiman Hakoō	一満箱王
Ichimura Hanzaemon	市村羽左衛門
Ichimura Takenojō	市村竹之丞
Ichimura-za	市村座
ichiya-zuke	一夜漬け
Iga Heinai Zaemon	伊賀平内左衛門
iki	粋
Ikyū (Hige no Ikyū)	意久（髭の意久）
Imagawa shinobi-guruma	今川忍び車
ima no Sukeroku	今の助六
Inoue Harima-no-Jō	井上播磨掾
Itchū Bushi	一中節
itsu-tateme	五立目
Izumi Tayū	和泉太夫
Izu nikki	伊豆日記
jidai	時代
jidai-mono	時代物
jo-biraki	序開き
Jōruri Gozen	浄瑠璃御前
Jōun	浄雲
Jūban-giri	十番斬
jūhachi-ban	十八番
Kabuki jishi	歌舞伎事始
kabuki no seimei	歌舞伎の生命
Kachidoki homare Soga	勝鬨誉曾我
Kagami-yama	加賀見山
Kagekiyo	景清
kaidan-mono	怪談物
kakikae	書替え
Kamachi Hyōgo-no-kami Akimune	蒲地兵庫上鑑連
Kamakura Gongorō	鎌倉権五郎
kamban	看板

Kampera Mombei	かんぺら門兵衛
kao-mise	顔見世
kao-mise sekai sadame	顔見世世界定め
katashiro	形代
Katō Bushi	河東節
Kawatake Mokuami	河竹黙阿弥
Kawazu no Saburō Sukeshige	河津三郎祐重
Keisei Kisegawa	けいせいきせ川
kenka no hachimaki	喧嘩の鉢巻
Kenuki	毛抜
kigo	季語
Kikeba mukashi Soga monogatari	聞伴昔會我物語
Kimpira jōruri	（金）公平浄瑠璃
kiri-kyōgen	切狂言
ko-jōruri	古浄瑠璃
Kokon kyōdai tsuwamono Soga	古今兄弟兵曾我
Kokuritsu Gekijō	国立劇場
ko-nadai	小名題
Kondō Sukegorō Kiyoharu	近藤助五郎清春
ko-shōgatsu	小正月
Ko-sode Soga	小袖會我
koten ni chūjitsu	古典に忠実
kōtō-mukei	荒唐無稽
kōwaka	幸若
Kudō Suketsune	工藤祐経
Kugami no Zenji	久上禅師
kumadori	隈取り
Kumasaka monogatari	熊坂物語
Kurodegumi kuruwa no tatehiki	黒手組曲輪達引
Kuruma-biki	車引
Kusazuri-biki	草摺引
kyōgen	狂言
kyōgen o tateru	狂言を立てる
kyōgen-tsukuri	狂言作り
Kyō Sukeroku shinjū	京助六心中
machi-yakko	町奴
mae-kyōgen	前狂言
mai no hon	舞の本
mai-osame	舞納
maki-bure	巻触
Mankō	満江

Matsunaga Teitoku	松永貞徳
matsuru	祭る
Meiseki Soga	銘石會我
mie	見得
Minamoto no Raikō	源頼光
Minamoto no Yoritomo	源頼朝
mi-tateme	三立目
Miura no Katakai	三浦の片貝
Miyako Dennai	都伝内
Miyako Itchū	都一中
Miyamasu	宮増
Mochizuki	望月
modoki	もどき
mono-mane kyōgen-zukushi	物真似狂言尽
Morita Kan'ya	森田勘弥
Morita-za	森田座
Moronao	師直
Motomasa	元雅
mukimi	むきみ
mu-tateme	六立目
Nagawa Kamesuke	奈河亀輔
naimaze	綯い交ぜ
Nakamura Kanzaburō	中村勘三郎
Nakamura-za	中村座
Namiki Gohei	並木五瓶
Namiki Shōzō	並木正三
Narita-ya	成田屋
Narukami Fudō Kitayama-zakura	鳴神不動北山桜
nembutsu	念仏
nempyō	年表
nendaiki	年代記
nenjū-gyōji	年中行事
Nenriki yatate no sugi	念力箭立杉
ni-bamme kyōgen	二番目狂言
ni-ban tsuzuki-kyōgen	二番続狂言
nigi-mitama	和御魂
Nimaze no ki	烹雑の記
ni no kawari kyōgen	二の替り狂言
nuregoto	濡事
Nyūgatei Ganyū	入我亭我入
Ōe	大江

Ōeyama	大江山
o-giri	大切
Ōguchiya Gyōu	大口屋暁雨
o-ie kyōgen	御家狂言
Ōiso no Tora	大磯の虎
Okina	翁
Okina-tsuki go-ban-date	翁付五番立
Okina watashi	翁渡し
Okumura Masanobu	奥村政信
Okuni	お国
omo-tadashii-mono	おも正しいもの
ō-nadai	大名題
o-nagori	お名残り
Oniō Shinzaemon	鬼王新左衛門
onna kabuki	女かぶき
Onoe Baikō	尾上梅幸
Onoe Kikugorō	尾上菊五郎
Ō-Soga Fuji kari	大曾我富士狩
Osome	お染
otokodate	男達
Otoko-moji Soga monogatari	男子文字曾我物語
ō-zume	大詰
rufu-bon	流布本
Saigyū	才牛
Sakata no Kintoki	坂田公（金）時
Sakata Tōjūrō	坂田藤十郎
Sakurada Jisuke	桜田治助
Sakurai Tamba no Shōjō Taira no Masanobu	桜井丹波少傢平正信
samban tsuzuki-kyōgen	三番続狂言
Sambasō	三番叟
Sankatsu	三勝
san no kawari kyōgen	三の替り狂言
Santō Kyōden	山東京伝
Sasagawa Rimpū	笹川臨風
satsuki	五月（皐月）
Satsuma Dayū	薩摩太夫
sekai	世界
sekku	節句
jinjitsu	人日
jōshi	上巳
tango	端午

tanabata	七夕
chōyō	重陽
Semi no nukegara	蝉のぬけがら
Sendai-hagi	先代萩
Sennichi-dera shinjū	千日寺心中
Senshūraku	千秋楽
Senzai	千歳
sewa	世話
sewa-ba	世話場
sewa-mono	世話物
shibai nenjū-gyōji	芝居年中行事
Shibaraku	暫
Shichi-fukujin	七福神
shichi-henge	七変化
Shichi-jū-ichi-ban shokunin uta-awase	七十一番職人歌合
Shiinomoto no Saimaro	椎本才麿
Shikirei yawaragi Soga	式例和曾我
Shiki Sambasō	式三番叟
Shimbei	新兵衛
shinji-bon	真字本
Shinshōji	新勝寺
Shintorigoe igyō-in	新鳥越易行院
Shiratama	白玉
Shirazake-uri Shimbei	白酒売新兵衛
shiri-metsuretsu	支離滅裂
shite	仕手
Shitennō	四天王
Shitennō osanadachi	四天王稚立
shizome	為初
shōhon	正本
shomin	庶民
shosagoto	所作事
shukō	趣向
Shusse Kagekiyo	出世景清
Shuten Dōji	酒呑童子
Soga matsuri	曾我祭
Soga monogatari	曾我物語
Soga no Gorō Tokimune	曾我五郎時致
Soga no Jūrō Sukenari	曾我十郎祐成
Sugawara denju tenarai kagami	菅原伝授手習鑑
Sugawara no Michizane	菅原道真

Sugiyama Shichirōzaemon   杉山七郎左衛門
Sukeroku   助六
Sukeroku kuruwa no ie-zakura   助六廓の家桜
Sukeroku yukari no Edo-zakura   助六所縁江戸桜
tachi-mawari   立廻り
Tadanobu   忠信
Tadanobu mi-gawari monogatari   忠信身替物語
Taimen   対面
Takasago   高砂
Takemoto Gidayū   竹本義太夫
Takenuki Soga   竹抜曾我
Takizawa Bakin   滝沢馬琴
tate   立て
tate-sakusha   立作者
Tate-suji yoko-suji no koto   堅筋横筋之事
Terako-ya   寺子屋
tōji   湯治
Tokugawa Iemitsu   徳川家光
Tominaga Heibei   富永平兵衛
Tomokirimaru   友切丸
Tora Gozen   虎御前
Tora no Shōshō   虎の少将
tōshi-kyōgen   通し狂言
Tsūrikibō   通力坊
Tsurugi sandan   剣讚談
Tsuruya Namboku   鶴屋南北
Tsuuchi Jihei   津打治兵衛
Tsuwamono kongen Soga   兵根元曾我
tsuzuki-kyōgen   続き狂言
Uji Kaga-no-Jō   宇治加賀掾
ukiyo   浮世
Ume no Yoshibei   梅の由兵衛
Urabe no Suetake   卜部季武
Usui no Sadamitsu   碓井貞光
Utagawa Toyokuni   歌川豊国
Wada sakamori   和田酒盛
Wada Yoshimori   和田義盛
wagoto   和事
wakashu kabuki   若衆かぶき
waki-kyōgen   脇狂言
Watanabe no Tsuna   渡辺綱

yado-sagari	宿下がり
yamabushi	山伏
Yamamura-za	山村座
Yanagita Kunio	柳田国男
Ya no ne Gorō	矢の根五郎
Yaoya Oshichi	八百屋お七
yarō kabuki	野郎かぶき
yatsushi	やつし
yayoi	弥生
Yorozuya Sukeroku shinjū	萬屋助六心中
Yoshihide	義秀
Yoshitsune	義経
Yoshitsune sembon-zakura	義経千本桜
yo-tateme	四立目
Yo-tsugi Soga	世継曾我
Yo-uchi Soga	夜討曾我
Yunzei yome-iri Soga	弓勢嫁曾我
Yuranosuke	由良之助
za-gashira	座頭
zatsu-kyōgen	雑狂言
Zenchiku	善竹
Zenji Soga	禅師曾我

MICHIGAN PAPERS IN JAPANESE STUDIES

No. 1. Political Leadership in Contemporary Japan, edited by Terry MacDougall.

No. 2. Parties, Candidates and Voters in Japan; Six Quantitative Studies, edited by John Creighton Campbell.

No. 3. The Japanese Automobile Industry: Model and Challenge for the Future?, edited by Robert E. Cole.

No. 4. Survey of Japanese Collections in the United States, 1979-1980, by Naomi Fukuda.

No. 5. Culture and Religion in Japanese-American Relations: Essays on Uchimura Kanzō, 1861-1930, edited by Ray A. Moore.

No. 6. Sukeroku's Double Identity: The Dramatic Structure of Edo Kabuki, by Barbara E. Thornbury.

Printed and bound by CPI Group (UK) Ltd, Croydon, CR0 4YY

13/04/2025

14656505-0005